PRAISE FOR
THE STROKE ARTIST

"Young Dr. Choate had it made. At thirty-five, he had survived medical school and a long residency, and it was time to start living the Good Life and pay off his student loans. Then, something happened inside his skull and the music stopped. He had suffered a massive stroke. It wasn't fair. Some writers are good at putting words together but don't have good stories to tell. Others have good stories but lack the skills to tell them. Bevan Choate has both, and this is a very fine book about experiences that most of us pray will never happen. I read it at one sitting. Well done, Dr. Choate!"

—**JOHN R. ERICKSON,** author of the Hank the Cowdog Series

"Readers of the Western genre are sometimes surprised and very much entertained by writers who bring their life experiences to pen and paper. From Edna Ferber's *Giant* to McCarthy's, Kelton's, and McMurtry's sweeping sagas, the storytellers of the West have given the reader an honest approach in writing about life's ongoing obstacles and struggles. Soon to be counted amongst them will be this young son of a Texas rancher, who becomes a doctor, a painter, and now a novelist . . . Bevan Choate. This short self-penned story, *The Stroke Artist*, speaks to all who have at one time or another faced and then overcome life's unplanned obstacles."

—**ALLAN HARRIS,** jazz vocalist, guitarist, and songwriter from Harlem, New York

"It was a privilege to read this book. Many passages are unforgettable. A test of great writing is whether the reader cares about the character(s) depicted in the book. I like Dr. Choate."

—**PERRY FLIPPIN,** former Editor Emeritus of *San Angelo Standard-Times* newspaper

BEVAN CHOATE, MD

THE
STROKE
ARTIST

a memoir

RIVER GROVE
BOOKS

This book is a memoir reflecting the author's present recollections of experiences over time. Its story and its words are the author's alone. Some details and characteristics may be changed, some events may be compressed, and some dialogue may be recreated.

Published by River Grove Books
Austin, TX
www.rivergrovebooks.com

Copyright © 2022 Bevan Choate, MD

All rights reserved.

Thank you for purchasing an authorized edition of this book and for complying with copyright law. No part of this book may be reproduced, stored in a retrieval system, or transmitted by any means, electronic, mechanical, photocopying, recording, or otherwise, without written permission from the copyright holder.

Distributed by River Grove Books

Design and composition by Greenleaf Book Group and Teresa Muniz
Cover design by Greenleaf Book Group and Teresa Muniz
Front cover art by Bevan Choate

Publisher's Cataloging-in-Publication data is available.

Print ISBN: 978-1-63299-513-1

eBook ISBN: 978-1-632990514-8

First Edition

To Eleni

My wife, my love, and the fire of my being.

Without whom I may have not survived to write this book.

CONTENTS

Introduction	1
1. A Brief Origin Story	3
2. For Whom the Hell Tolls	7
3. Brass Tacks	13
4. Getting to Know You	17
5. Cerebellum? Never Knew 'Em	21
6. The Calm and the Storm	27
7. The Vivid World	37
8. Peewee Germans	41
9. La Madrona	45
10. A Not So Decent Proposal	51
11. Blue Lagoon	55
12. Office Hours	57
13. Tears of the Salt Mine	59
14. Clinical Espionage	63
15. Tipping Point	67
16. The World Seen Through Your Own Prison	71
17. A Convenient Complication	75
18. Preparing for War	79
19. Game Time	83
20. From Sundown to Thumbs Up	87
21. Don't Go Toward the Light!	95
22. Act Natural	101

23.	Greener Pastures	103
24.	Awkward Nudity	107
25.	Brian	111
26.	Rebooting the Brain	113
27.	Jeepers Peepers	115
28.	New Roomie	117
29.	Eyes on the Prize	121
30.	The Greatest Escape	125
31.	A Joyous Homecoming	129
32.	My Lovely Wife	133
33.	The Prodigal Parents Return	137
34.	The Fears of a Ruminating Mammal	141
35.	Back to School	145
36.	Restored to Default Settings	149
37.	First Comes Love	153
38.	Honeymoon in DFW?	159
39.	Getting to Work	163
40.	Painting	169
41.	An Unforeseen Complication	173
42.	Momma B	179
43.	Flying the Coop	181
44.	Meanwhile, Back at the Ranch	183
45.	Clear for Takeoff	189
46.	Looking Outward Means Looking Inward	193
Acknowledgements		201
About the Author		199

INTRODUCTION

After discussing the recovery and prognosis of my stroke with my dear friend and urology colleague, he suggested I write down an organized chronology of the details and events surrounding this truly shitty occurrence. He said this exercise might be therapeutic and something to reflect on later in life. He said some events may even be funny in retrospect, although I wasn't laughing at the time. However, I decided to give this a shot, if only in order to try to retrain myself how to type using a left hand that had become foreign to me. After all, practice makes "potentially better." Becoming normal again, whatever "normal" had been, was in no way a guaranteed outcome.

1

A BRIEF ORIGIN STORY

I was born in San Angelo, Texas, in the summer of 1985. I grew up in a family consisting of a sister, five years my senior, and my mother and father, who've now been married for forty-eight years. My childhood was standard American middle class. Compared to the modern day, I'd go as far as to say my childhood was Rockwellian. My dad's brother and his family also lived in San Angelo, and both families spent a lot of time at the family ranch about fifteen minutes northwest of town. It seemed that money was always tight. My grandfather and dad ran a cattle-trading company out of the relatively small ranch, and much of my childhood was spent on horseback, moving, sorting, and doctoring cattle in relentless heat.

My granddad, Wade Hampton Choate, was my hero. He had survived the Great Depression and joined the Navy during World War II at age sixteen. That's right. Sixteen. He bent the rules with some doctoring of his own and escaped poverty to join the war effort. He learned a good deal in the Navy and taught me how to weld at nine years old. Sadly, he died on a New Year's Day while I was in medical school.

My dad made it clear to me at an early age that he did not want me to go into the cattle business. He said it was too difficult to make a living at cattle-trading in the modern era. For this reason, and to hammer the point home, my dad and granddad gave me the most vile work they could, like cleaning filthy water troughs and digging manure out of the cattle guards. They refused to teach me to steer rope because they didn't want me to catch the cowboy bug you hear about in all those country-western songs.

I spent a lot of time on the ranch, often doing all-day jobs with workers from Mexico who didn't speak a lick of English. I admired their work ethic and demeanor despite being obliged to perform what I thought to be backbreaking work. Perhaps that admiration is what drove me to want to learn Spanish and travel to Spanish-speaking countries later in life.

I did well in school, as did my older sister, who proved to be a damn good role model. She was the star of the family. A nationally ranked tennis player who graduated among the top ten of her high school, she somehow also managed to be a high school party legend. She earned a full-ride scholarship to play tennis for the University of New Mexico.

I was competitive. I had to be better. I had an "Aha!" moment in the tenth grade and put academics and the pursuit of knowledge at the forefront of my aspirations. I buckled down and graduated number three of 787 students in my senior class. Like my sister, I, too, was an avid partier. I went to the University of Texas at Austin on a partial academic scholarship, where I roomed with a cousin of mine. Only a little over 200 miles—about a three-hours drive—from San Angelo, UT Austin was kind of the go-to state school for that region of Texas, and many of my best friends went there as well. Most of us did well in school, despite partying our asses off. We even pooled our resources and bought a used sailboat so that we could party on the Colorado River or up on Lake Travis. I realized about midway through undergrad that I wanted to be a doctor. I was always a science geek at heart and figured medicine to be a pure and noble application of science.

I ditched my chemistry major to pursue a degree in Spanish, as I'd already completed most of my pre-med requirements. I figured, why not earn a useful skill from academia? I was paying them enough. So, from there, I learned basic Spanish and traveled to Mexico and Argentina as much as I could. I knew immersion was the only way to become truly fluent in and adept at another language. From what I could gather at the time, study abroad programs were bogus and mostly for rich kids who wanted to go on vacation with their parents' money. I wanted to be better. It paid off, as speaking Spanish gave me a huge advantage in caring for and speaking with patients in Texas and New Mexico.

I excelled in medical school and completed my five-year urology residency in Albuquerque. It was the roughest five years of my entire life. Being a sleepless subordinate for almost two thousand days is a tough pill to swallow. Nonetheless, I persevered and began practicing urology in Albuquerque. It was my calling. I loved it. I loved my patients and some of them even loved me. I did quite a bit of oncologic surgery and got good at robotic surgery using the Da Vinci robot. After years of hard work, I had finally come into my own.

2

FOR WHOM THE HELL TOLLS

I awoke December 3, 2020, to my phone's alarm clock music of Agent Orange at 5:55 a.m. I was next to my sleeping, beautiful—then fiancée, now wife—Eleni. The desire to urinate compelled me to uproot myself from the cozy spoon drawer of my king bed and start my morning routine. Mumbling a declaration of my intent to Eleni, I took one step out of bed and toppled to the hardwood floor like a bar-style Jenga tower, knees and elbows flying akimbo. The room was spinning out of control. Tears in her eyes and perplexed, Eleni helped me up onto the edge of the bed.

The unyielding vertigo soon caused me to violently vomit a thick, yellowy acid onto the floor, as my stomach was mostly empty. Eleni placed a large white mixing bowl beneath me, and I retched my guts into it for two more minutes until I was able, finally, to lie back onto my side. In an effort to stop the incessant spinning of the room, I closed my eyes. It helped but did not address the cause of the problem, whatever that might be.

Eleni is a very sharp family physician, and we both were mentally working through differential diagnoses of what felt, to me, like a demonic possession, and must have looked as such to her. I must be experiencing the symptoms of benign paroxysmal positional vertigo (BPPV), we concluded. Oversimplified, BPPV is a disorder caused by dislodgment of inner ear crystals that regulate your head's perceived position in space. Crystals—that must be it. Eat your hearts out, naturopaths. Symptoms include vertigo and vomiting. We had decided on a benign and thoroughly treatable diagnosis that probably indicated more humanistic hope than medical diagnostic skill.

I ate a strawberry-flavored meclizine chewable and tried to take a short nap. The vertigo, if anything, was worse upon waking and I continued the vomit-retching into my large bowl. *Poor bowl*, I thought. *You were designed for kneading bread, but today you are being used for something far less inviting.* My wife pleaded with me to let her take me to the Emergency Department.

Being the stubborn surgeon, I of course refused and remained in denial that my acute illness was anything more serious than the flu. Surgeons don't get sick. We retire in our sixties and then we die. I was only thirty-five as this phenomenon was occurring! Eleni appealed to my training and ability as a physician, ultimately convincing me I could potentially develop kidney failure due to the copious amount of fluids I was losing by vomiting.

After another testosterone-fueled refusal, followed by still more retching that could not be refused, I caved, and together we headed for the nearest ER. The walk to her car was perilous at worst, a visual spectacle to entertain neighbors and passersby at best: a one-hundred-pound, petite lovely creature gamely shouldering a lumbering two-hundred-and-five-pound man swaying and rocking like a palm tree in a hurricane. The short one-hundred-foot journey was painful and difficult. To avoid the hospital COVID protocols, we drove to a pop-up ER.

The staff met me at the car and plopped me into a wheelchair. In the ER, the physician in charge put me through the treatment protocol again for BPPV. My condition had not improved. The ER doc asked if I wanted a CT scan of my head. I was hesitant but I muttered, "Sure." Actually, I was terrified, because by agreeing to the CT scan, I had tacitly abandoned the notion that this was a short-lived, reversible malady. Going from the ER bed to the CT stretcher was a serious challenge.

I performed a sort of rotational flail from a quadruped position onto the stretcher that seemed to amuse the techs and nurses. Some laughed under their breaths. Others, not as polite, laughed out loud. Later, I added a butt-mooning through my hospital gown. At the university hospital, upon stretcher transfers, I would declare a rare sighting of twin albino turtles. I knew one of the techs at the university imaging facility and did the butt-mooning transfers to mess with him in front of his colleagues. It worked and provided some much-needed comic relief. I would say, "Quit looking at my ass, pervert!"

The CT scan was performed professionally and without incident. Shortly thereafter, the ER doc entered the room to give us the news we had been dreading. There was a large hypodensity in my left cerebellum. At that instant, it felt as though the ground beneath my feet fell out from under me. I hadn't even thought about a neurological cause but even I knew this meant I had suffered a stroke. This wasn't fair. How the hell could this have even happened?

The next thing I knew, I was talking to an Indian neurologist via Zoom from my ER bed. His accent was quite thick, and his summary of the bad news drowned me in wet cement. He asked me what I did for a living. I replied frankly yet pitifully that I *used* to be a urologist. He chuckled, then essentially told me something to the effect of *don't say that. Chin up!* "You still are!" he cheerfully assured me. In that moment, it was hard to believe that a return to normalcy would ever be within reach.

After a twenty-minute ambulance ride, I found myself in the university hospital ER trauma entrance. The university hospital is one of the few centers in town qualified to provide the level of care required to manage stroke patients. I was strapped into the transport gurney and wheeled into one of the trauma bays. On the way in, many familiar and unfamiliar faces greeted me with smiles that only faintly hid their deep concern for my condition.

As I'd been a urology resident at the university almost three years prior, I still had friends and acquaintances there. Some came to say hi, and some came to simply rubberneck and look into the face of too-young bad luck. In the trauma bay, Jordan—a general surgery resident and close personal friend of mine and Eleni's—came to visit me and stayed at my side in the room. I owe a debt of gratitude to her and to her husband Trevor, both of whom worked tirelessly behind the scenes, above and beyond the call of duty, to help keep the cogs of our lives moving during the worst time of my life. They even took care of my certifiably insane dog.

There was a brief moment of calm after the pain of what I'd learned—a moment of such extreme helplessness that there was no other option than to take solace in the pain. It was a lot like tasting your own blood after a fight. It's not good—it's quite bitter in fact—but it centers you as a human, beast, or competitor in life. You're not sure why it happened, but it did. Time to dig in and suck what little water from the roots you can before dehydration, fate, or the cold hand of God takes the reins.

3

BRASS TACKS

In the trauma bay, I remembered that I had not urinated since shortly before going to bed the previous evening at around 9:00 p.m. I told one of the nursing techs in my bay. I was concerned with this duration of not peeing as I feared I would earn myself a Foley catheter. I requested a bedside urinal as a basin in which I could try to pee. "Bedside urinal" is a fancy name for a simple hospital device. It is the well-known rectangular plastic urine receptacle with a forty-degree bend at the top for patients to pee in while in bed. I could not urinate despite my focused efforts.

For over three decades, I had always successfully urinated standing upright. As kids, we used to pee off my cousin's deck to see who could stream the farthest. Now it was unsafe to stand, much less pee, in that position. After failing volitional urine voiding, the nurse tech suggested a condom catheter. A condom catheter is exactly what it sounds like. It fits over the penis just like a condom, though the tip is a hollow tube that couples to a drainage tube and collection bag.

Jordan had fortuitously left the room at this point. I awkwardly placed the condom catheter over my recalcitrant member with my only functional hand, in front of the male tech and female nurse. Genitalia are a large part of my career, and of course peeing comes pretty natural to all of us, but the hovering of two nursing staff members was off-putting to my suddenly bashful bladder.

Having been on their end of healthcare just a short time ago, I realized I had generally acted just like them. It had not been uncommon for me to pull up a patient's gown, abruptly and without warning, to quickly check an incision on rounds, even if their genitals were exposed briefly. In my present case, they needed to make sure I could get the thing on.

In that moment, I realized I had become numb to what my patients feel in similar situations. I rationalized that "This is just medicine. Procedures must be performed, progress checked, and we can't wait around forever." Now that I was the patient, I quickly learned to appreciate the importance of preserving modesty and maintaining my patients' dignity.

I made several ultra-focused attempts at urinating into the condom catheter tubing. I was able to eject a few short bursts of pee, but I never truly got anything going. It was now 3:30 p.m. on December 3. I still had not peed. I felt like I was being punished for being a urologist and that karma had reared its ugly head. I knew the worst was coming. In my mind's eye, I could see the faces of every old man cursed with a pathologic urethra I had ever catheterized. Visages aglow with vengeance. Rows of elderly faces smiling at my current affliction and reveling in my anguish. Schadenfreude.

4

GETTING TO KNOW YOU

Hours passed and after several neurologic exams from nameless providers in the ER, I was wheeled into my neurosurgical ICU room. I later found out that this was the result of the intervention of a hospital higher-up. A colleague of mine had spoken with one of the hospital administrators and this had expedited my assignment to a room in the appropriate ICU.

At the time, this was the ICU least afflicted with COVID. I admit that finding this out made me feel privileged and special, and anxious as I was to find a resolution to my current affliction, any "movement" whether physical or investigatory felt like I was making progress in the right direction. But I also felt rather guilty that most people don't have the same opportunity. I had witnessed patients in the larger ERs sometimes having to wait up to forty-eight hours to be taken to their appropriate hospital rooms. Even with special treatment, four hours of staring at the harshly bright lights in the ceiling had felt like an eternity.

My skull pounded like a snare drum wound so tight it would rip, but the pain was masked by the fear of the unknown. Would I make it out of here alive? Would I ever be a surgeon again? Would Eleni leave me? Would she break off our engagement? My thoughts began to spiral in the darkest way. I felt useless to the world and scared I would never return to the life I had worked so hard to create.

By the time I was placed in Room 6 of the neurosurgical ICU, it was dark outside. Not that I would have had any way of knowing it. It was dark throughout the entire NSICU. The ICU had no windows, but I felt the darkness outside. The ICU was deliberately kept dark inside for the comfort of the many light-averse neurosurgical patients. To me, the light was a menace for other reasons. My turgid, painful head felt marginally better with closed eyes. Closing my eyes was also the easiest way to cope with my now constant double vision. And closing my eyes was a way to avoid, psychologically I guess, the new reality that I believed was my likely dour future.

A parade of physicians, residents, advanced providers, and nurses in the ICU came through my room. They asked about my deficits and did various iterations of the same neurologic exam. For example, they had me try to touch their finger, then my nose. Right-handed, I was perfect. Left-handed, I would miss their finger entirely and smack my hand into a nurse's face or an IV pole. My left arm and hand were completely beyond my motor control. This symptom was not good news for a surgeon.

5

CEREBELLUM? NEVER KNEW 'EM

Based on my presenting symptoms and deficits, I had a combination of an anterior inferior cerebellar artery stroke (AICA) stroke and a posterior cerebellar artery (PICA) stroke. All of this resulted from an intimal dissection—or internal shearing of my left vertebral artery. The same artery you hear horror stories about being torn during chiropractic manipulations. Fortunately, this rare and identifiable trauma accounts for only forty percent of cases. I had never been seen by a chiropractor and can't point a finger—especially the fingers on my left hand—at any cause. Bad luck.

If one imagines the human brain as a woman's hairstyle, the cerebellum resembles a ponytail bun. It sits behind and underneath the right and left brain (the cerebrum). It is the part of the brain that coordinates and refines intentional movements and helps us maintain balance and fine motor skills, like picking up a dime off a smooth flat table.

A neuropsychiatrist once told me that the cerebellum is a new frontier in brain research because so much is still unknown. Our cerebellum makes up roughly half the neurons (the functional units) in our brains. It allows our movements to be fluid and natural and makes good dancing possible. It also automates our movements so that we don't have to think about activating each specific muscle group in order to walk or wave goodbye. Additionally, it maintains our equilibrium and helps our eyes move in tandem to track and fixate on objects.

It is also the overlord of proprioception. Proprioception is our brain's concept of where our body is and how it moves through space. Some people view proprioception as if it were a sixth sense. Without proprioception, we would not be able to walk down a crowded sidewalk while texting without crashing into at least ten people. We wouldn't be able to drive a car or brush our teeth with the affected side's hand. Fortunately (if only marginally so), my left side was affected, and I am right-handed. However, until you have lost it, you don't realize how frequently you use your weaker hand.

I told my nurse, a fellow named Jaxson, that we were approaching twenty-five hours without peeing. It was 10:00 p.m., and I knew my bladder had by now suffered a "stretch injury." A stretch injury of the bladder occurs when the muscle layer of the bladder is stretched by radial distension from the increasing volume of accumulating urine to the point where it can no longer squeeze and contract for peeing. People normally avoid this by urinating six to eight times per day.

However, my new normal that would dictate my future as a functioning human kept me sewed up in my own head. Taking a piss was simply not at the forefront of my "to-do list" that day. As a result, I paid the price and a bladder ultrasound performed at bedside showed "> 999 milliliters." The bladder scanner ultrasound machine reports "> 999 milliliters" as the maximum amount it can detect in a urinary bladder, as it is not manufactured to detect any higher number. The treatment is the same regardless. There was way too much urine in my bladder.

The average full bladder in a person can hold roughly 400 to 600 milliliters of fluid. For reference, a pint of beer is about 473 milliliters. I needed a Foley catheter in the worst way, and that is how I was going to get it. A Foley catheter is a dreadful device made of a latex or silicone tube that is passed through the urethra and into the bladder to keep the bladder continuously draining by gravity. Once the fluted tip of the catheter is in the bladder, a balloon surrounding the tip is inflated to keep the catheter from falling or sliding out of the bladder.

Despite having placed thousands of catheters in my short career without a second thought, I nevertheless feared receiving one. Part of me couldn't wait to have it placed while another part of me dreaded the thought. My bladder was tense and beginning to hurt like hell.

Once the kit was prepared and the tip of my penis was cleaned with betadine, I decided to give the nurse some pro-tips about catheter placement. A master class, if you will. After all, most of my requests to place catheters were the result of nurses attempting but failing to correctly make Foley placements. I have always been keen to educate. Sometimes out of kindness, sometimes for want of not being called again in the middle of the night. The greater the skill these nurses achieved, I reasoned, the fewer trips to the hospital for me.

To be fair, they are usually attempting catheter placements that the doctors ostensibly supervising their duties are too cowardly to do themselves. I told Jaxson to make a lower-case "a" with the first three fingers of his left hand and to pinch my penis just behind the head. I demonstrated in the air. I then told him to place my penis on outward stretch and to grab it like it was his. "You're not gonna hurt me," I lied. I explained that this straightens the urethra for easy passage of the catheter.

He looked at me like I was selling him a timeshare. He then rammed the latex catheter into my penile urethra having utilized exactly none of my advice. It torturously jabbed and jangled its way through my urethra at every internal nook and bend. It felt, I imagined, like someone had deployed a TASER inside my penis. I wanted to wring his neck when he told me no urine was returning from the tube. "Keep advancing the catheter," I groaned. "You've stopped at my sphincter." I took a deep breath and one more painful push brought yellow gold. Two liters (the equivalent of four and a quarter beer pints) eventually drained from my no longer bloated bladder. I did not feel much better after this, but I was glad to no longer be worried over my urologic perils for the time being.

I had eaten the elephant one bite at a time and at least the acute issue had been surmounted. I realized that my male nurse was probably not very psyched to place a catheter in a urologist. It would be like me caddying for Tiger Woods. I know how to play golf, but Wood's caddy could still probably beat me by forty strokes. I ultimately told him "good job" and that he did great. It was a bald-faced lie, but by this time I was figuring I needed all the friends I could get.

The nurse was a nice guy and I appreciated what he was going through to care for me. However, in such a setting, I'd take competence over "being nice" any day. But what could I do? I was at the mercy of my new reality. Thus, at least a small part of me had to appreciate the irony of this terrible event that put me in such peril. The rest of me remained in an out-of-body state of incredulity, watching a cruel fate unravel in slow motion. What would become of me?

6

THE CALM AND THE STORM

I finally got to sleep that night around 11:30 p.m. The day had been a living hell. Alarms with seemingly no apparent function beeped in random intervals. Nurses and technicians came in and out of my room, moving like panicked squirrels in a city park. I awoke at 6:00 a.m. the next morning still in disbelief that I had experienced a stroke. I quietly prayed I would wake from one of my morning cat naps neurologically intact, and that this was all one big cruel dream. A few residents and attending physicians from the urology team stopped by to say hi and see how I was doing. Seeing them evoked poignant nostalgia and melancholy.

These were my fellow soldiers. I could barely hold a conversation. I sobbed uncontrollably. My mother called and I could no longer keep it together. Conversations were pointless, as I couldn't go three seconds without crying. It was as if suddenly I had realized how precious the joys of life truly were, and mine were being taken from me. It was hard to see myself this way. It was devastating to think that others could see me this way. Pity is not my thing.

For the remainder of the day, my vital signs and exams were monitored closely to make sure the stroke was not producing too much swelling and pressure on my brain. Excess pressure within the cranium is dangerous. Adverse effects can include headaches, vomiting, high blood pressure, precipitous slowing of your heart rate, and breathing changes. In severe cases, it can displace parts of the brain and cause instant death. It was not at all clear that I was not one of those severe cases.

Concerns over increased intracranial pressure required a repeat CT scan. I mooned the CT technicians in the usual fashion getting into my CT bed. The bed, by design, loaded me into the CT gantry like a torpedo. I concede that for the claustrophobic, a CT gantry feels more like a coffin, but it was comforting in the moment. I was finally left alone. I felt at peace in the room's quiet sterility, devoid of noise and medical personnel. I thought about the vastness of the universe. Was there another timeline out there wherein I didn't have a freak stroke? Would that Bevan still be out there perfecting his craft and becoming a better surgeon by the day? The calm pondering drove me into a deep sleep.

Later, I woke up to the neurosurgeon telling me the pressure on my brain had increased. He recommended a bedside placement of an EVD. EVD stands for "external ventricular drain." It is usually placed at a location in the frontal bone of the skull known as Kocher's point in order to divert cerebrospinal fluid (CSF) and thus lower intracranial pressure. Ventricles in the brain are like cisterns that house CSF. The EVD can also be used as a barometer to measure internal cranial pressures. As I explained it to my best friend, "they put a straw in my coconut" to take the pressure off my brain.

After I signed the consent form, the surgeon gave me an 80s punk rock haircut that made the Flock of Seagulls' haircut look tame. I felt the cold antiseptic as he prepped the surgical site atop the right side of my skull. The surgeon then injected a syringe full of lidocaine with epinephrine into my scalp and the soft periosteum covering of my skull. I could barely feel the incision of the small scalpel on my scalp exposing my skull. But I could certainly hear the horror-film-worthy cutting and scraping of the knife. It sounded like a pack rat readying its den in a tin-roofed barn.

A power drill was next used to penetrate my skull. Again, I heard more pack rat scraping. Finally, the drain was carefully placed within the space between my skull and brain. The drain was secured to my head and I felt accomplished that I had survived becoming a Capri Sun while awake.

Placement of the EVD was an outright eerie experience. It was not painful. I was expecting to have to show the neurosurgeon how tough I was, but it never really came to that.

I was warned during the consent process that the EVD may not be successful. It was not, and by late that day I found myself signing another consent form. On December 5, I was taken to the OR to undergo a decompressive craniectomy. In other words, they cut out a piece of my skull to create more room for my brain. I survived this surgery and was returned to my ICU room.

Over the next few days, they continued to monitor me closely. My memory of this time period is fuzzy; I'm guessing because it seemed routine or boring to me. Time itself, when not punctuated by appointments or events or the experience of movement from one point to another, becomes fuzzy and untethered, fluid yet meaningless. Of course, it could also have been that I was hopped up on narcotics and/or that I'd had a massive stroke, both of which may have been messing with my cognitive awareness and memory. We may never really know.

Though things had become relatively routine for me, Eleni was fighting a war from home. She was moving the remainder of her things into our home one morning when a social worker from the hospital called with power of attorney questions. Unbeknownst to me, my parents had sent legal documents to the hospital for Eleni to sign that would relinquish power of attorney control to them. I would not learn of this until much later, but I'm eternally happy that Eleni didn't concede. To this day, I've never confronted my parents about it. I'm guessing that they decided to proceed in this manner in fear that Eleni would jump ship and leave me. She was thirty-two, with a whole life ahead of her. We barely knew each other's families. Eleni and I had developed most of our relationship during the COVID pandemic. At the time, we were merely engaged and had no children. There was nothing legally binding us. Regardless, I remain thankful that my loving wife remained in my court. She is a physician and speaks physician. She had a detailed understanding of what was happening to me and could make complex medical decisions that most people could not. I don't think I hyperbolize when I say I might be dead if it were not for her. Her actions still speak to me about our commitment and love to one another. Eleni felt belittled by my parents' actions and was hurt by the underhanded manner that things were done. I cannot blame her. I would have felt the same in her shoes.

Eleni would later tell me that, around this time—and by the way, much of what I "know" about "around this time" is based on what Eleni has told me because I was too out of it to experience these events for myself—I developed signs of pneumonia. I was retaining too much carbon dioxide in my body due to poor breathing. The poor breathing was a result of high intracranial pressures and, to a lesser degree, narcotics for post-surgical pain. This spiraled into Acute Respiratory Distress Syndrome (ARDS), a pathologic process that severely curtails normal breathing and has a mortality rate of 40 percent. I am glad I was too gorked out at the time to have processed what those four letters mean. Ignorance was indeed bliss.

The ICU team then tried to maintain my condition by intubating me and putting me on a ventilator. Being treated amidst a backdrop of the COVID pandemic, more people know about ventilators than they'd ever hoped.

Over the next few days, I remained on the ventilator in an effort to keep my oxygen saturation up while my pneumonia was being treated. A bronchoscope is a medical device that has a tube with a tiny camera on the end, which is inserted through the mouth into the lungs. My doctors performed a bronchoscopy. The purpose was to drive a camera into my lungs and take saline-lavaged (washed) cultures to identify any offending organisms. My delightful little cultures grew out MRSA.

MRSA stands for methicillin-resistant *Staphylococcus aureus*, a type of bacteria that is resistant to most antibiotics. I had pneumonia from the Michael Jordan of bacteria. Apparently, Pseudomonas also grew out, which also happens to be a formidable bacterium with at least Scotty Pippen status. *Pseudomonas* bacteria, too, are constantly finding new ways to evade the effects of the antibiotics used to treat the infections they cause. As infections go, I was about as sick as you ever want to be in a hospital if you are still hoping to walk out.

Accordingly, I was continued on exceptionally heavy intravenous antibiotics. By the weekend, things had gone from bad to worse. On deck in the CT scanner area, my heart rate suddenly dropped by over half. My breathing slowed and my blood pressure increased out of the blue. This phenomenon, known as Cushing's Triad, is a harbinger of bad things related to increased intracranial pressure. My doctors administered atropine to bring my heart rate up, then wheeled me emergently to the operating room.

The neurosurgeon was no longer putting on bromides of hope with Eleni when they spoke over the phone. He knew that Eleni was a physician and simply told her that the pressure on my brain was increasing dangerously and they needed to take me back to the operating room STAT. STAT is medical speak derived from the Latin word *statim*, meaning instantly or immediately. You get the picture. He had a frank discussion about how the situation was no longer routine and that my operation may result in permanent neurologic deficit or even death. There wasn't really a better alternative, but I admire the strength of my wife for giving the go-ahead. I could not legally or practically consent as I was sedated with a tube in my trachea. Her courage in a bad situation likely saved my life.

Quickly, I was prepped and taken to the OR. The plan was to go through the prior incision and remove a section of the infarcted cerebellum to create more space and reduce pressure. More plainly stated, a large portion of the left half of my cerebellum had died due to loss of blood and nutrients from the obstruction, or blood clot, caused by a sheared arterial lining of my left vertebral artery. This damage created a beaver dam in the artery, causing turbulent blood flow and clotting. The now clotted dam then choked off several minute arteries that fed my left cerebellum.

Clots that block the brain's tissue from getting nutrients and oxygen cause that tissue to die. In my case, as in many others, the death of that tissue caused inflammation and swelling within a finite volume—my skull. With no place for the pressure to go, an EVD was placed and it failed. Next, a piece of my skull was removed, and this too failed. I was now on the third-line fix. There were not a lot of options after this.

After the surgery, I was alive and well again (if "well" might be defined as pertaining only to my fundamental vital signs), though I came out of the OR with a breathing tube remaining in my throat. If my head were a C-23 cargo plane's hull, the surgeons had in effect opened up the plane's rear door and torn it off. This is what I imagine every time I rub the upper entry way with my pointer finger. The precious cargo still bulges out the bottom, especially after I've been sleeping on my back throughout the night.

Despite an excellent surgical result, there were too many variables preventing safe removal of the breathing tube. I was being treated for a serious pneumonia, and a significant portion of my brain had just been melon balled. I needed a backup in the event I stopped breathing, which was still a very real possibility at this point. One false move surgically, or further pressure on my brain stem, and my breathing would have no longer been automatic. A few days later, they would perform a bedside tracheostomy on me. This is a breathing tube that is placed directly through an incision of the throat's trachea below the vocal cords. It is commonly placed when someone has been conventionally tubed through the mouth for an extended period. I would remain on the ventilator with a tube T-boned through my trachea for twelve more agonizing days.

ICU psychosis is a very real thing. In order to keep someone from freaking the hell out, waking up, and yanking all the tubes out of their necks, it is commonplace to sedate patients. Sedation for intubation generally involves infusion of a low continuous drip of medications intravenously that keep you in a sleepy amnestic state.

It makes sense: who the hell wants to carry forward the memory of having had a lung-fingering machine breath for them? They had me on the Conrad cocktail (so named for its criminally negligent application by one of Michael Jackson's personal physicians) of propofol and fentanyl for the majority of the time—properly administered in my case, of course. When I was being a really bad boy on the vent, they added some Precedex to round me out and keep me from Hulking.

7

THE VIVID WORLD

The sedation, while necessary, gave me vivid hallucinations and dreams that I still struggle to regard as not having actually happened. In the "Vivid World," I walked, talked, and could use my left hand adeptly as if I hadn't had a stroke. Even a month later, during the first forty-eight hours or so after stopping my sedation and removing my breathing tube, I found myself returning to the Vivid World.

In Vivid World, I am a sort of protagonist in a role-playing video game, yet in a dream-state. Sometimes I would progress within a scenario for what felt like hours or days. Other times it felt like just a few minutes. That is, when time as we know it seemed to pass at all. In one of these scenarios, I succeed in "ending racism" in the world. Some of my friends who have known me to be somewhat of a "no catch 'em no eat 'em" Libertarian thought this was rather funny. I tend to think more in terms of "content of character" than I do about race. In the dream, the means to achieving this noble end is obscured by sedation logic or rather a lack thereof. My explanation of this is clear as mud.

Vivid World begins when I learn that I was adopted by an American couple in Tanzania, where I was born. Odd, as my parents are from Texas, where I was born, though they did work for US Aid in Tanzania in the seventies. US AID at that time was a lot like Peace Corps. I was born in 1985 and I look as if my father had undergone mitosis to form me. No DNA test needed to establish my paternity.

In reality, I have not a single gene from my tanned and beautiful mother and look about as African as Doogie Howser, MD. It's clear now that the dream is bogus but after returning to the real world, it still seemed as gospel. I can't explain it any better. I woke up thinking I had won a Nobel Peace Prize and had loads of book deals and money accruing from my "selfless gift to the world." What a contradictory concept!

I promise I am not a self-important asshole. Please consider that I entered Vivid World upon consuming sedation for an entire month. Back in Tanzania, I found myself living in an Adobe-like mud hut on a hillside. I was at my biological mother's house. She was a gaunt, Maasai-looking woman whose smile lit up a room.

She spoke to me in Swahili and I had no problem conversing with her. I don't speak Swahili. My real-life parents did, at least while they lived in Tanzania. My mother told me I was to live with her in her village for a week. I did everything to help her keep the household running. I herded cattle with the men of the village, hand-plowed the fields behind a team of oxen, and regularly walked steep hills to a well to retrieve water.

A few much younger siblings were still running around the house. I even met one of my younger brothers, Asheli, who had just returned for the weekend from Nairobi. He was a young physician as well, working in Kenya. Asheli had a dark complexion but looked exactly like me. One of my younger siblings, whose name I can't recall, looked like me but had albinism and was quite pale. After about a week had passed, I asked my mother who my father was. She said he had left their small village about five years after I was adopted by the American couple. He had moved to the capital to work a high-profile government job.

After I returned from my Africa—that is, my Vivid World version—I searched the internet and found my biological father. He clearly had albinism and was some higher-up political figure of the Tanzanian government. Part of what my friends thought was funny about this fantasy was that I believed an African male with albinism and a black African woman made a Howdy Doody-looking white boy. After reviewing my medical texts and Punnett squares, having an albino African child is very possible from said parents. Having a rangy hayseed like me, well, that just evades science.

At any rate, my albino biological father was an instrumental figure in the negotiations that ended apartheid in South Africa. He was a big deal. He had a Wikipedia page and I can only remember that we shared the first name "Bevan." This was a groundbreaking epiphany for me. I had a Eureka moment in Vivid World. It was an exhilarating feeling. I called my adoptive parents and they confirmed my findings. In Vivid World, I somehow became instantly famous. I was famous by association. I was no better than a Kardashian, but I remember feeling like my success was merited in the warm, fuzzy embrace of the Vivid World. I made my rounds on talk show circuits. I spoke at college graduations. I had a following and was already getting book offers before a manuscript was even written or conceived.

Somewhere between Vivid World and waking, I knew my hospital bills would be exorbitant and perhaps insurmountable. In addition to this unexpected shit show, I had at least an extra hundred grand to pay off on my medical school loans. It didn't matter. I was gonna make millions off the book deal. I still can't fathom how the sedation and narcotics made me both a realist and a surrealist at the same time. Furthermore, how "fame by association" made sense to a surgeon who busted his ass to get where he is, I still cannot comprehend. I suppose even in normal dreams we can fly.

8

PEEWEE GERMANS

Another bizarre Vivid World adventure was not so warm and fuzzy. In fact, it was downright nightmarish and nauseating. In this life, I was a commander in the waning days of World War II and in charge of a ground battalion of British troops. The catch, though, was that the troops were males between the ages of four and seven years old. Even in the Vivid World, I petitioned higher command to stop this madness, but they assured me they were of an acceptable age for armed combat and that both England and Germany had massive shortages of adult soldiers. I was told something to the effect of same guns, smaller targets, better press. The "battlefield," as I recollect it, was bizarre.

The British side was a large grassy meadow divided longitudinally by a shallow creek and bordered on the east by a 20-foot-high wall–type dwelling that separated us from the Germans. The wall dwelling housed our anachronistic Chinese aerial ammunition.

The Chinese missiles were essentially oversized black powder bottle rockets. You would light them and throw them by the sticks over the walls to engage in mostly percussive harassment. I don't think they were capable of killing a stray fox.

The eeriness of it was how tormenting war felt. It was a mix between helplessness and impending doom. Almost like my current lot in life. Fortunately, I never saw kid warfare in the Vivid World. The biggest catastrophe on the battlefield for me was that I accidentally left the artillery vault unlocked and the German kinder stole a good deal of our Chinese missiles overnight. I was officially reprimanded but was not discharged.

Instead of playing Red Rover with armed children, back and forth against Hitler's youth, my sedated subconscious took a different route. It chose to try its hand at more of a prequel love story, perhaps out of fear of poor viewership with the whole child soldier angle. I was on a hillside in Allied Territory, still in the Second World War next to a delivery ward/soldier production facility. My wife Eleni and her friend Jordan were assiduously working this delivery ward to earn "study abroad" medical school "extra credit" and global goodwill.

They were helping deliver the Allied babies. It was an assembly line. After delivery, the "term" babies, AKA the ones born on time, were greenlighted through and transferred to the war effort. The term babies aged before our eyes to the appropriate four- to seven-year-old size to start life as soldiers and were sent immediately to the front lines. They were given "vitamins." The preterm or premature babies had a slightly different fate. Upon delivery, they were encased in river clay and placed in coal-burning ovens to be rapidly incubated to account for lost developmental time within the womb.

They came out looking like chocolate Easter babies you might buy in line at the drugstore. I helped Eleni and Jordan "hatch" the clay-covered preemies by cracking their cocoons with a ball-peen hammer and pulling them free. They were then sent to join the term babies in the "war effort."

Eleni was beautiful and unassuming in the Vivid World. She is, in fact, the most beautiful woman I have ever seen and as a result she looked no different in the Vivid World. We briefly talked shop about the atrocities of war but carried on as if we were already married. I loved her and she knew it. Even in Vivid World, I knew I was nothing without her.

As I mentioned, Vivid World to me was as real as taxes. When Eleni was finally able to visit me in the recovery hospital, I asked her if any of the babies being hatched ever showed burn marks from the hot clay. She looked at me like I was crazy. I was. At least temporarily. It was only then that I began to conjecture that Vivid World may not actually exist. Probably never existed.

9

LA MADRONA

Yet I lived another adventure in Vivid World somewhat closer to home, a little more believable, though almost as disturbing as the "children's crusade" of World War II. It started when I awoke in a hotel room alone and bound to the bed by my arms. This was probably my mind's translation of the "soft restraints" they had placed on me in the ICU to prevent me from pulling the ventilator tube out of my trachea. The hotel room was about as nice as an airport Hilton. The duvet was quality down with a high-thread-count cover. It was a nice place to wake, but I could have done without the restraints. I was terrified by the thought that even if someone knew I was in danger, they wouldn't know where to find me. After what felt like two hours of intense struggle to wrest myself free of the restraints, I escaped and attacked the minibar. I furiously rooted for a ginger ale. I found a twenty-ounce bottle and chugged it down. The crisp, sweetly chilled nectar rushed the receptors of my mouth and gullet and drove me to a brief moment of ecstasy.

For about five seconds, waking up in an anonymous hotel didn't seem so bad. But after the ginger ale wore off, the terror set in once again. I called the front desk to ask where I was. A woman answered and she said she was sending someone up, but she never answered my question. I climbed back in bed and fastened my wrists back into the restraints to make it seem like nothing had changed in case my captor(s) returned. Two hours passed and no one came to my room. I again wriggled free of the restraints.

Three housekeepers then entered my room and began furiously cleaning the room. I froze and held completely still. They looked right through me as if I wasn't there. I firmly stated, "Buenas! Cómo están? Dónde estámos? En que pueblo estámos ahorita?" They didn't acknowledge me and continued cleaning and talking amongst themselves in Spanish. No sooner had they entered, than they were gone again. I still hadn't a clue where I was, but judging by the pictures of ski slopes on the walls, it seemed like Colorado or northern New Mexico.

The hotel room was lit in an eerie manner. I could not discern the time of day or night. I found a Polaroid picture sitting on the kitchenette bar near the telephone that I hadn't noticed before. I picked it up and immediately studied it. The photo was of my dog

Indi, except she was not the way I left her. She was sprawled out on a concrete floor stained with puddles of blood and looked as if she had just lost a fight. Her neck was matted with saliva and blood, and she was missing the tip of her left ear. The most terrifying aspect of the picture was when I looked very closely and discovered that steel talons apparently had been surgically fused to Indi's front paws. I swallowed my heart.

I was so sad for my dog, but at the same time I was palpitating with juggernaut rage. I tried cooling my head. A few deep breaths brought me no closer to calm. But I was in survival mode and had that keen alertness to remain unfaltering and to do things one step at a time. I knew that if I submitted myself to blind rage, I might end up the next dog-fight contestant. After confirming that my keys and some cash were in my jean pockets, I walked the motel hallway to the exit sign and alighted outward from the eerie building.

A dusky sunset assaulted my eyeballs despite the relative low light. The temperature was crisp and clean. I found my real-life silver pickup truck parked in a space of the hotel parking lot under a Ponderosa pine near a dumpster. I started up my truck and made my escape. I drove away fast and reckless, as if I had stolen it. This marked the end of this episode. In Vivid World, I knew more terror was to come but I had somehow departed for the time being.

I was then transported to a square pier in a small canal somewhere in Europe. The most striking aspect of this place was how deep blue and calm the water in this canal was. It was Prussian Blue, the glasslike surface barely undulating in a way that was almost imperceptible. Incomprehensibly, the canal was multitiered and it had several shops built up onto piers. I apparently was an antique dealer in one of the shops, and it was second nature for me to take clients on the shop tour and tell them the history of any item of interest. The sun beat down on the piers and felt comfortable in contrast to the bleak and icy appearance of the water below. This place would come to be remembered as some purgatory or temporary place of respite. I blinked and it was gone.

I woke up again in a nondescript hotel room. This time I was not bound to the bed frame. The sheets and comforter were so similar to the previous hotel that I knew it was from the same ownership, but it was not the same place as before. After raiding the mini-fridge and downing the ginger ale, I looked around for clues about where I was and could find none. I walked outside to the parking lot again and this time I didn't find my truck. The lot was mostly empty. However, I was near a town plaza.

I wandered through the quaint mountain town and stopped at an art gallery. I asked the owner where I was. He and the out-of-towners behind me in line looked at me, perplexed. He said we were in Pleasant Grove, Colorado. I am not sure if that is a real town or not, but based on the shopkeeper's description, this particular Pleasant Grove was near the New Mexican border. Looking back, it was probably some brain-warped rendering of Antonito.

As I wandered the streets of this town, people stared me down with intense scrutiny. Despite walking normally in Vivid World, I did still have a bandage and a bang-up, avant-garde shave job on my dome. Basically, I was a fish out of water. In addition, I was probably the only person walking around alone. I tried walking at a steady, confident pace, as if I had some destination in mind. It was useless. I was out of place. They knew it. I knew it.

I walked up to a road that appeared to be a highway. A defunct train track bisected it near the town's southern limit. It ran east-west. Based on the sun's position, the highway was definitely headed south. I recall thinking the only trains I had ridden in my life ran east-west and how this was peculiar but largely uninteresting.

I walked for what felt like hours before I was picked up by a New Mexico state trooper. His name plate said Hernandez. He was overweight with a crew cut and was nicer than I expected. I told him what had happened regarding the stroke, my mutilated dog, and the weird hotel thing. I overheard on the trooper's radio that I was six miles south of the Colorado-New Mexico border.

After an hour or so of driving, I was taken by the police to a hospital of sorts in Española. I underwent the intake evaluation with mostly nurses and techs. They focused heavily on neuropsychiatric questions and barraged me with memorized questionnaires. It became clear that I had been taken to a psychiatric ward—AKA, the loony bin.

My worst fear came true. I was now a prisoner based on false pretenses. In retrospect, the thing that sucked the most about nightmarish times in Vivid World was the permanence of it. You can wake yourself up from a nightmare when you're asleep. If things get too heavy, most people can hit the "eject" button and wake up.

You can't wake up when you're sedated. That's kind of the whole point of sedation. Furthermore, in dreams, a lot of times we realize that we are in fact "in them." Why else would we attempt flying or try to keep from waking up from a good dream? As I said before, Vivid World to me was undeniably real. It felt as real and true as me sitting down to write this book.

10

A NOT SO DECENT PROPOSAL

In this Vivid World episode, I finally spoke with a psychiatrist who wouldn't make eye contact with me. I explained that I was a physician. He didn't hear me. I started to shout, "I SAID..."

"I heard what you said!" he interjected. He made it clear that he wasn't going to level with me. He went through his lists and checked his boxes. I maybe got three words in edgewise.

I was then placed alone in a mostly bare room. It looked like a depressing prison bunk room. An hour later, in walked a middle-aged Hispanic woman in non-hospital attire. She reminded me of the actress that played Selena's fan club manager in the late nineties movie that was watched in every Spanish class in Texas ever. She made the hair stand up on the back of my neck. She introduced herself but I still cannot remember her name. "La Madrona," a nickname repeated by her henchmen, was the only name I still recall.

She said she knew who I was and that she was a very powerful woman in New Mexico. She said if I so much as mentioned dog fighting or kidnapping, she would make sure my dog and I were dead. From her lengthy soliloquy, I gathered she rolled in some tough circles and hid in plain sight. I learned that she owned a Tex-Mex restaurant chain in New Mexico and the Texas Panhandle, along with a handful of luxury motels from Burque to Pagosa Springs. "Burque," by the way, is a slang abbreviation for Albuquerque.

It then dawned on me that it was in her motels that I had woken up the previous times. I cussed her up and down and told her she wouldn't get away with this bullshit. I threatened to kill her once I got out and told her how I'd do it. I was raging mad. She disagreed and faked a laugh. "Look if this is about the ginger ales . . ."

"Hijo de puta! Cállate la boca!" she yelled. "I have big plans for you, so you had better listen up."

She told me she had friends in the police from Santa Rosa to Farmington and that if I agreed she would get me out of this prison within the day. I weighed my options. I figured I had a better chance escaping a delusional psychopath than I did the Española's finest. I nodded okay.

She left and my room lights were turned out. I eventually fell asleep on my sheetless loony bin couch-bed made of foam rubber. I was awakened just before dawn and carried outside the facility walls and placed into a large van. The men that carried me out were large and dangerous-looking Hispanic men in their early forties. One had multiple tattoos on his face and neck. He had done time for sure. I was taken to a trailer house in the middle of nowhere.

I was placed on a foldout couch in the living room and seated in front of La Madrona. I asked her why she'd killed Selena. With a nail file from her purse, she stabbed me through the web of my left hand, which was resting on my knee. Amazingly, it did not penetrate my thigh but certainly hurt like hell. She told me to shut up and pay attention. She explained that she had emancipated me from the police for a hefty down payment.

She said from now on, I was to be her "go-to doctor." She told me that now that I'd had a stroke, I would be useless as a surgeon and might as well hand over my resignation to my employer. She told me flat out the dire finances I'd be in in a few months after a mountain of medical bills and no job. She told me I was to be her enterprise's personal physician.

My job would include refuting disability and workman's comp claims from her restaurant and hotel employees who had gotten hurt on the job. I would also be prescribing narcotics to her black-market dealers and intermediaries.

Furthermore, she was going to bankroll me to run a medical marijuana clinic. This way she would be able to have a legal supply of marijuana to sell on the streets *and* have another profitable business to add to her busy portfolio. She would pay me a salary of $100,000 to keep up appearances, pay malpractice insurance, and maintain credentialing.

She would pocket the remaining lion's share, which by her estimation would be $700,000. It was a win-win for her. I was now chained to a crazy bitch's entrepreneurial whims. Regardless, I was happy to be out of that depressing loony bin full of cons and drug addicts. I was on my own.

Six weeks had passed since my freedom had been bought and flipped by Selena's fan club manager. She was a real piece of work. Regardless, it was nice to at least pretend to be free and see patients, even if they were mostly college kids and small-time pot dealers with "anxiety and chronic back pain." It made the days pass and I eventually didn't think about killing la jefa every second of every day. "La jefa" is Spanish for "the boss," and she never let us forget it.

I began to wonder if I hadn't caught a case of Stockholm syndrome. After all, if it weren't for her, I'd be drooling over a plate of sedatives in a human kennel in upstate New Mexico. I hated handing her the bulk of my profits at the end of every month, but then again, better a crook here than a crook in DC.

11

BLUE LAGOON

I returned to blue lagoons and talk shows for what seemed like a week. I grew pretty tired of it. Fame is cool and everything, but being famous in a dream I guess is a lot like being unremarkable in the real world. It just didn't have the same bite. The only thing new of this was that I found out my antique-dealing, purgatorial headquarters was on the Greek coast.

12

OFFICE HOURS

As advertised, la jefa told me I would be rejecting her workers' disability and workman's comp claims by falsifying medical reports and saying they were good to get back to work. At that point, she would usually fire them. Most injuries were as follows: falls on a kitchen floor slick with aerosolized fry grease or inhalational injuries from cleaning supplies. I was just as mad at the old cow's workplace negligence as I was at the workers for letting it continue. I mean, damn. Change the record already.

I returned to this Vivid World nightmare and found myself in my clinic on a Saturday morning. I was seeing ten patients who were employees from the hotels or restaurants. Some had driven hours to see me. La Madrona forced me to hold office hours for workman's comp and disability evaluations on Saturdays. It was also a sort of general walk-in clinic for her employees. Most of them were Spanish-speaking patients with terrible or non-existent health insurance. My copay happened to be zero dollars for restaurant and hospitality workers. As a result, I ended up seeing a few walk-ins from one of the city's rival underworld firms.

La Madrona didn't seem to care that I saw them, as turning people away might have raised some questions that neither she nor I wanted to answer. They were mostly henchmen without documentation or eastern Europeans owned and employed by Italian boss Vito Catoni. His legitimate business was a speakeasy-themed restaurant. Talk about hiding in plain sight.

Mr. Catoni was a portly Italian with a large head and sausage fingers, his cheeks like an English bulldog. I had eaten at his restaurant in my previous life. Albuquerque doesn't have many restaurants worth writing home about. I remember thinking way back then what a kitschy caricature of an Italian place it was. The food was so-so.

I always liked seeing these eastern European underworld types, though. They were fighters who had overcome quite a bit of circumstance with nothing more than an eighth-grade education and two fists. They were mostly men between the ages of eighteen and thirty and dressed like they came out of the nineties. They had all broken their noses at some point and they all wore mullets: business in the front, nineties democracy in the back. They looked like movie extras in the filming of the Berlin Wall's destruction.

13

TEARS OF
THE SALT MINE

That same day I saw a Panamanian woman named Griselda. She had come to America sixteen years ago and had recently married a Mexican man named Santos who ran a backhoe for a developer in Rio Rancho. He was naturalized some years back. She was around forty years old. "Dime lo que pasó," I said. "Tell me what happened."

She said she was cleaning up a room at the motel in Chimayo when she dumped her used chemicals in the bathtub as she always had before. She returned to the room before heading out to confirm it all drained. It had not because the stopper had been left in the drain by the previous occupant. She went to pull up the stopper mechanism, and a deep breath sent her to the floor coughing and retching. She had clearly mixed some ammonia with a bleach-containing product inadvertently and inhaled the chlorine gas byproduct.

She could barely talk she was so short of breath. It would be a long time with a lot of pulmonary rehab before she would ever work again. I reviewed her most recent X-rays. Her lungs looked bad. The "read" from the radiologist said something like parenchymal shadows with bilateral infiltrates and patchy interstitial markings. That's radiologist-speak for "looks like dog shit."

I felt for her. I knew that even on two incomes they were struggling to get by. The school system in Burque was rough. They were plenty religious but also wanted better for their kids and thus they were sent to a private Catholic school. A lot of people in Albuquerque did this out of necessity. I couldn't write a fake note.

I put in her medical record the appropriate findings. She didn't deserve any worse. She was a really good person. The following day I came clean to La Madrona. I told her what I did. I figured she wouldn't mind a blip on her insurance premiums. Boy was I wrong.

She unloaded. Apparently, she didn't like her pocket doc scribbling outside the lines. The last time I saw rage like that was when I spilled Jell-O on a Hispanic kid's new white socks in ninth-grade gym. She let me have it. She hit me with every cuss word in the book and put me in my place. The sad thing was that she was pretty well right.

I had grown too big for my britches. She reminded me that she bought me and still paid the EPD monthly to keep me in a white coat and out of a straitjacket. Nonetheless, her obstinacy hit me like a solar flare. I wanted to kill her. I wanted real freedom. I wanted to get back to my real life. Talk shows and social justicing would have done if the first option was off the table. I just wanted out of this seemingly inescapable hell. She made me retroactively alter Griselda's chart to deny her claims and dispute the findings. I felt sick to my stomach. I had no choice.

14

CLINICAL ESPIONAGE

The following Saturday, I held my usual office hours and saw mostly Vito's Iron Curtain outlaws. No less than four of them had gotten into fights the night before and needed someone to sew up their eyes, chins, or mouths. It was a fun morning. I enjoyed getting my hands bloody. They said it was the MS13s or some other equally unimportant group of Rhodes Scholars. It was all too exciting for these East bloc goonies. They wouldn't shut up about how good they whipped up on them.

The last guy I saw was named Janus (Yah-noose). He was a regular. He always wanted antibiotics for a sinus infection. He was a tiny Jewish hypochondriac in a Strongman champion's body. He was, for all intents and purposes, the leader of the ruffians. Janus had a speech impediment and a poor command of the English language, which made the fact that he was a chatty-Cathy even funnier.

I love walking ironies. He must have been in his late twenties and was from somewhere like Latvia or Azerbaijan. He was a "wild and crazy guy." He was a good dude despite his day job.

Janus and I would usually talk soccer or exchange secrets about La Madrona. He was always pumping me for information on the bitch, probably on Don Vito's behalf. In answer to his probing questions, I gave him the same vaguely inconsequential "not much" every time. I was her property, not her priest. I knew probably less than he did. He asked why I looked so tired. I told him I couldn't sleep.

He kept asking me oddly specific questions about La Madrona's health. Like if she had been to the hospital lately and when she had gotten out. Rather than question him, I just sort of played along. I made up some dates, times, and fake diagnoses. I said she was hospitalized for a pneumonia for about four days. He said, "Neh-oo-monia? I thot it vuss her kitneez failink?" I corrected myself and countered with an "oh yeah, you're right." I made up something about how I confuse patients all the time and that it was another of my patients that had the pneumonia.

I told him I hadn't had my coffee this morning. No sooner than I muttered this worn-out expression, I realized he wouldn't get it. He didn't. I continued this pleasant disinformation game with Janus and learned that La Madrona was diabetic. From the history provided by my glib friend, I pieced together that she was a type 1 diabetic. Even better.

I hadn't known this about my vile captor. Different from the much more common type 2 diabetes mellitus, type 1 diabetics usually require injectable insulin to manage their blood sugar levels. Many have trouble keeping their blood sugars tightly controlled with insulin even in the best of circumstances, and they often develop chronic end-organ damage. Common end-stage damage tends to affect organs like the heart, kidneys, and eyes.

Apparently, her kidneys were taking a hit. Even if she developed fulminant kidney failure requiring dialysis, she still might live another three to ten years without a kidney transplant. I didn't have that kind of time.

15

TIPPING POINT

That night I had gotten home to my trailer park abode, living quarters that I was given as a prior courtesy of La Madrona. Most of her "help" lived in this park. Her goons lived amongst us to keep tabs. At least I had a double-wide with cable and internet. The door was slightly ajar.

I always locked it whether I was inside it or not. Disturbed, I cautiously snuck in and opened every cabinet and closet in the tiny dwelling to confirm no intruders. I had my pocketknife out in stabbing position. I didn't find anyone.

On my kitchenette bar, I found an unsealed manila envelope. I opened it up in a frenzy. It contained some photos that I dumped out onto the plastic countertop. The first three were pictures of Eleni pushing a shopping cart in a parking lot. The last two were pictures of my dog. She was dead and lying on her side with matted blood covering her neck and ears. She had a bullet hole in her side. I couldn't think. My vision went red and I wanted to burn the world to ashes.

I wanted every living thing on Earth to be dead. I wanted to rain fire from the sky. Those were pictures of my wife. That was my dog. I was ready to kill and ready to die. When I would get this way in my previous life, I would need to beat my punching bag until I felt real pain or completely tired myself out. I punched four holes in three cabinets before I was cool enough to think.

I grabbed a bottle of Irish whiskey from the fridge and finished the last of it. I told myself I wasn't a pathetic cretin. "You're a fucking wolf," I yelled as I beat the counter with my fists. I belted out a curdled yell until my vocal cords felt like blood and glass. One of the goons rushed in and told me to shut my mouth.

I pretended like I wasn't fazed and told him thank you for stopping by. I then went into a flow state of focus. Enough was enough. I went to sleep that night half-drunk and maybe slept an hour before I was yanked out of bed by three large goons with pistols. They ordered me to get dressed. I demanded they hit the START button on the coffee maker.

It wasn't worth the pistol whip to the side of my head. That woke me up. Regardless, I grabbed a twenty-ounce to-go mug full of black coffee and chugged it down. They drove me to my clinic office. The lights were on and there were three trucks parked in the lot. They walked me in, prodding me in the back with the muzzles of their pistols.

The oldest one, Lalo, asked me if I was ready for surgery. "What are you talking about?" I asked.

I was tired of these "men" pushing me around. I grew up in San Angelo, Texas. I'd seen how Latin men were raised. Most of them were coddled mama's boys.

Somehow, I oughtta be able to take advantage of this and overcome. I was thinking to myself what I was going to do. Did they mean they were going to cut on *me* for my recent transgression? I calculated an escape. There were now five guys with guns in the room. No way I was getting outta there without a bullet in my back, then head.

When I saw what was awaiting me in the procedure suite, the pieces all suddenly fell into place and I knew what was going on. There was a dead man lying supine on a metal table in the procedure suite. He looked to be a medium-build, short Hispanic man in his mid-fifties.

I knew the bitch wanted a kidney and this was probably a relative or someone that died and had a directed-donation advanced directive to her. At least that's what I told myself. I was being ordered at gunpoint to harvest a dead man's kidneys by the *Vatos Locos*.

Every one of them had a gun pointed at my head. They told me to hurry up and I heard mutters in Spanish that La Madrona was prepped and already under anesthesia. Much to the goons' astonishment, I checked for breathing and pulses and confirmed he was dead. I was not going to be an accessory to murder in addition to a black-market organ harvester.

As I unzipped the dead man and entered his abdominal cavity, I could hear the cocking of four pistols and a pump-action shotgun. I worked feverishly. "Apúrate! Apúrate güero!" they shouted. I opened up the chest, vented the right atrium, and cannulated the aorta to slam in the UW solution. UW solution is the liquid used to preserve human organs for transplant, developed at the University of Wisconsin, which is why it's called UW solution. They had all the necessary equipment for this procedure, oddly enough. I was impressed. La Madrona had more connections than I gave her credit for. I took down the white lines of Toldt and entered the retroperitoneum. Within twenty more minutes, the kidneys were out and in a cooler.

"Bien hecho, puto," one of them said. Two of them left with the goods and boarded a helicopter outside. The men in the room had tattoos from tip to toe and had probably killed scores of people, but a few of them nearly lost their lunches looking at the tableau of viscera I had created. I was glad that these assholes would have the pleasure of cleaning up my abattoir.

I was satisfied with the kidneys' vein lengths and artery patches. It's probably a surgeon thing, but it's just not in our blood to do bad work. At least someone else would probably get a kidney out of this ordeal. At least that's what I told myself.

16

THE WORLD SEEN THROUGH YOUR OWN PRISON

The following week I caught a glimpse of La Madrona making her rounds. She was moving slowly. I noticed some dried blood on the right lower part of her shirt from the Gibson incision from her transplant. Shit. She would live another fifteen years at least, I thought to myself.

She looked at me briefly. Her body expressed disdain, but her face told me thank you. She got into the passenger seat of a brand-new Suburban and left. I inhaled deeply after holding my breath. I held back the Lake Mead of pure rage that brimmed inside me.

I would learn later that my situation with La Madrona in Vivid World was a lot like my new reality in the real world, even after four months of rehab. Standing still, I was a decent-looking young physician on the way to becoming a good surgeon. I spoke well enough and was a funny-enough guy. Throw a Nerf ball at me and it quickly becomes apparent I am broken. My power steering and camera-assist are gone. My left hand is a fish caught in the wild. I went from curing patients of cancer with a million-dollar robot to doing worksheets about Jenny's bake sale. In an instant, I had gone from high-functioning freedom to incarceration. Would it have been better to have died in ignorant bliss? This, I'll apparently have to find out later on.

My life in this nightmare board game was near perfect in many ways. I could walk, run, and jump. I could practice medicine, if you can call it that. I could drive my truck. Someone off the street may see me and say I had it pretty damn good.

In reality, I was a prisoner. A prisoner bound by the potential to harm myself or others. One wrong step in La Madrona's kingdom, my wife may be killed. One wrong step off a sidewalk in the real world, I may be back in the hospital getting my CAT scanned and my pecker rammed.

At the beginning of my therapy, a lot of counselor types prodded me for "how I was doing with everything?" Code for: *Are you planning on killing yourself or others*? I truly was able to answer them with a genuine "I'm great. Just looking to get on with the next steps." Based on grief stage theory, I was in the Denial Phase.

It was liberating and was the best I had felt throughout my awake recovery. Both myself and others didn't expect much from me at this point. It was simple. Keep moving forward and onward or you die. I was a shark.

17

A CONVENIENT COMPLICATION

Speaking of cold predators, La Madrona called me up to meet her at the clinic. I met her there in the evening. The fading sun no longer had any warming effect on the high-desert chill. Getting into my clinic was like getting into a big city nightclub. There were goons dressed in black at every step with Radio Shack nonsense in their ears.

One guy's belt displayed a small grenade. I came upon her, La Madrona I mean, in the procedure room. She was sitting on the edge of the procedure table. Her gown was stained with pink serous fluid. She said she had recently had a kidney transplant, of which she was sure I was aware. I nodded in acknowledgment and started putting on gloves.

She explained that since a day ago she had been oozing a pinkish fluid from her incision that wouldn't quit. She then let me examine her incision after lifting her gown. I cautiously lowered the right top of her granny panties to expose the extent of the Gibson incision. "They sewed you up," I said. "We normally used to staple these incisions. Who was your doc?" She said his name and I didn't recognize it. Sounded like some new hotshot, Dr. Slickman, that unknowingly did a thankless job. Sucker.

"Well, I have good news and bad news. You and your kidney are going to be just fine. You just have a seroma. It's not an infection. I'm gonna have to open it up and drain it or it won't ever quit." I explained it in terms she could understand. I told her not to worry and that with proper wound care, she'd have a good kidney and a funny-looking scar and nothing else to worry about. "We just now have to let it heal from the inside out," I told her.

I went to the "kitchen," as we called it in the clinic. It was a narrow room that contained all of my instruments, medications, and a crash cart. I grabbed lidocaine, a laceration tray, and a boatload of packing supplies. I came back in the room and prepped and draped the wound.

I reached for the lidocaine. "Bee sting," I said as I injected the areas to open with lidocaine. She winced. This made me happy. "Don't enjoy this too much," she said. "This hurts me more than it hurts you," I lied. After a brief pause, I reached for the scalpel. *Click, click.* Next was the unmistakable feeling of a gun's cold steel on the base of my skull. "Easy, champ," I muttered like a crazy person. "Can't cut without a blade." The goon backed off at Madrona's command.

I incised the bridges of skin that divided one large connecting wound. I used my finger to break up the loose internal adhesions of the wound, releasing a gush of clear pink fluid. I mopped everything up with gauze sponges. I packed the wound with half-inch sterile packing tape. "I'll need to change this packing daily, unless you wanna do it," I said. She declined and agreed with my plan. Perfect, I thought. I had an opportunity to get close to the beast.

The first week, we met at my clinic at 5:00 p.m. every day. I would remove the lightly blood-tinged packing in a perfunctory manner and replace it with a foot of half-inch, clean, saline-soaked packing. The simple wound care still hurt her so I used lidocaine to numb the wound edges. I acted like I would around any patient. I even pretended to treat La Madrona like a nice, normal person. I was never trained in medicine to judge a terrible person.

After a few weeks, she would just stop at my trailer and I would do the changes on my couch in the foyer with goon in tow. Another week passed of me doing trailer park wound care. Dammit, he's back, I thought. I figured the goon would eventually just wait in the car, but this never happened.

One night I found myself saying, "Does he really have to be here?" She replied, "I'm not as stupid as you think, Dr. Choate." This pissed me off. I needed to get her alone. Or did I?

18

PREPARING FOR WAR

That night I got in my truck and headed off the premises. As anticipated, I was stopped by the goons near the highway turnoff.

"Where you going, doc?" one said.

"Need to grab a bite to eat. Fridge is empty."

"Djoo neetah getcher seff an ole lady, cabrón."

"Báaaahahah!" they cackled.

"Wow. That's clever, Cantinflas," I muttered. They were in tears laughing like hyenas as I drove off onto the highway.

I drove to Blake's Lotaburger and bought a chocolate shake and some fries. I put my right index finger on the top of the straw to lock in the suction. I then dabbed a bit of shake to stain my beard and shirt. I strewed a handful of fries out on the passenger side seat to really let the greasy fry smell perfuse and set up in the cab. I was going to have to sell this experience later.

After I was done making a mess, I cleaned up the fries and took a long rip off the shake. I tossed the bag of fast food in the trash. I then drove to my clinic.

I went immediately to the "kitchen" and hit the light. I broke the tiny zip tie off the crash cart drawer. In the cart, I grabbed the injectable lidocaine and several vials of short-acting insulin. I emptied the lidocaine bottle with a draw syringe, leaving only about six milliliters of lidocaine. I filled the remainder of the 20-milliliter lidocaine vial with insulin until it was full to the gray stopper. I then dug through the crash cart and scrutinized the rescue medications in the corresponding drawer. Epinephrine. Perfect. I worked quickly, as about forty-five minutes had passed since I left the compound. I emptied the contents and replaced it with mostly insulin and put it back in the drawer labeled "Crash Cart Meds."

I replaced the miniature zip tie on the drawer to make it look untampered. I wore nitrile clinic gloves the whole time and threw them away once finished. I then drove back to base camp. As I pulled up to the checkpoint, I hit the cabin overheads and made sure to take a big swig of chocolate shake so the goons could see it. One of them did a once-over of the cab and looked in my eyes. "Your truck smells like fooood," he said.

"Yep, good ole Blake's." "*Chiiiiiinetas*, tengo hambre, güey," he said. "I'm hungry."

"Vete pa la chingada."

"Roger that!" I replied and took off down the dirt road toward my trailer.

19

GAME TIME

I barely slept that night. I couldn't shake the feeling of something sticking in my throat. Looking back, this was more likely a manifestation of the tracheostomy than a sense of guilt. The next morning, I went through my daily routine and arrived at the clinic at 7:30 a.m. I went through my day like any other. I got home that evening and waited.

La Madrona and her goonie walked up to my mobile home around 5:15 p.m. I got everything ready as I had so many times before. As per usual, the pleasantries were kept to a minimum, and I draped and prepped out her wound. She said, "Ya know, Doc, for as stubborn as you are, you do pretty good work." I thanked her and told her that her wound was healing up as expected. I told her it would be healed up in two more weeks.

I took the insulin-tainted lidocaine bottle and gripped it like a blood diamond. I used the draw needle to extract the contents into my syringe. I exchanged the needle for a twenty-five-gauge hollow-tip injection needle and began injecting along the edge of the wound in the manner I had done several times before. I made sure her goon was watching. I quickly changed her packing out and told her "All done." She told me this time hurt more than the last ones. "That's good. It means your nerves are coming back," I lied.

They loaded up and shipped out. I took a huge breath in, then out. I sat down on the sofa chair and put my clasped hands behind my head. I was taking a brief rest before the ensuing shitstorm. Ten minutes later, the suburban came tearing through my driveway spraying rocks into my door. The goon, frantic and distraught, ran to my trailer and nearly beat down my door.

"Doctor! Vénte vénte, cabrón! Es La Madrona. Se desmayó! Se está muriendo, güey! Vénte pinche cabrón!"

I acted alarmed. This was easy given I merely had to mirror the emotional state of the goon.

I ran with him to the Suburban and pretended to check her pulse. I told him to drive us quickly to my clinic as I had a crash cart and an AED there. He understood and we took off tearing through the serpentine dirt roads.

The goon was frantically calling the others to explain in unintelligible full-tilt Spanish that La Madrona was in trouble and that we were driving her to the clinic. An armada of pickup trucks and government-looking vehicles trailed behind, like a scene from *Mad Max*, kicking up plumes of dust and caliche. I kept trying to console the driver, saying I would do everything to save her, and for a moment, I believed it.

We hit the parking lot of the clinic. I helped the goon carry La Madrona into the clinic and we laid her on a stretcher bed. The goon pleaded with me to hurry and by this time a goonie audience was forming in the clinic suite.

I barreled into the room wheeling in the crash cart like a contestant in a supermarket spree. I connected the AED sticker paddles to her chest and visibly demonstrated to the helpless crowd that I was starting a CPR resuscitation protocol.

I tilted her head back and checked for breathing and pulses. Her carotid pulse was imperceptible from the digital artery in my pointer finger. Her breathing was faint and very shallow. I started chest compressions.

I made sure I was nearly making the back of her sternum crush her heart. I then worked my hands out laterally, cracking her ribs. I yelled for one of the goons to hold the bag mask over her mouth and to take over with the compressions while I switched places with him. I gave two breaths and ordered the AED machine to tell me if she had a shockable rhythm. She did not.

Perfect, I thought. *Time to bring this Oscar performance home.*

A few goons in the room were crying hysterically and I ordered them to get the hell out of there. I didn't want to see grown men cry, and I wanted to sell my degree of intention and focus by demanding no noise or hysterics. We were all about to lose our jobs. I needed the ones who could later talk to an investigator to see this.

"Doctor! Sálvala!" one pleaded.

"Traigame el carrito! Ahorita!" I replied. I told him to break the zip tie by quickly opening the drawer labeled *medicinas* and to grab me the epinephrine. "Epinefrina idiota! Dámela!"

I took the vial from him labeled "Epinephrine." I made sure everyone had heard what I said and that they could see the vial. I drew up its contents and injected it into La Madrona's antecubital vein.

Adios, puta, I thought. I did another round of fake chest compressions. She wasn't moving. I checked her pulse with a gesture of deep concern. Her pulse gently flickered like the flame of a candle taking its last breaths of air. I listened to her lungs. She wasn't breathing anymore.

"Está viva! Se está respirando pero poquito," I lied. I explained that we needed to get to a hospital immediately, or she would die. I knew at this point she would never affect my life anymore.

Even if she survived, she'd be unable to inflict any nonsense on anyone ever again. At best, she'd be a greeter at the city dump. I can't remember how I convinced them to get on board or what reason I used, but the troops mobilized, and we drove to the county hospital.

I only remember talking to a few police officers and several physicians. I was waiting to ride off into the sunset and go spend eternity with my young beautiful wife. I didn't get the chance. I woke up.

20

FROM SUNDOWN TO THUMBS UP

Just like on one of those dreamy TV afternoon soap operas, my hair was softly parted, lips slightly pursed, and my blue eyes beamed as the world welcomed me back from my month-long coma.

Wait, that definitely did not happen. To be honest, I cannot even remember waking up from sedation.

It's not a light switch. Nurses and physicians probably do a few math problems in their heads, but they mostly just wait for your body to metabolize the sedation after gradually turning down the drip to the point where you can hopefully stay awake. Not much different than sleeping off a drunken night, right? Not really.

They have to titrate these things slowly and safely so that you don't wake up and start tearing down the theme park they built around you while you were sleeping. I have no memory in this reality of the sedation-weaning period, which likely would have lasted a day or so.

Shortly after, Jordan came by and saw me sitting up. She asked me if I knew where I was, and I mouthed "No."

She asked, "Are you sundowning?"

I looked her in the eyes and gave her two thumbs up. The ICU nurse in my room laughed.

Sundowning is a term that describes hospital patients becoming delirious and whacked out for many reasons: age, being in an unfamiliar environment, not knowing the time of day, medications, and not having access to critical tools like glasses or hearing aids. In fact, Jordan had been obliged to recount this first conversational exchange some days later, after I came off the sedation; I do not actually remember mouthing "No," or sticking my thumbs up.

Jordan also later told me that, the next morning, I was desperately pleading with the nurse for a Sprite or a ginger ale. Jordan said I appeared hopeless after the nurse came back five minutes later stating no such beverages existed in the ICU. Jordan found it pretty amusing that by five o'clock I was drinking a Sprite. I am told that Brian, the X-ray technician I had mooned previously, had bought me a Sprite from the food court. I was proud of my porcelain-white ass.

Unfortunately, the next chapter of my life began in an intermediate hospital known as a Long-term Care Facility, or an "LTAC," as we call them. It's poorly named as I was there for only twelve days or so. I only truly needed to be there for about eight days, but it is fairly common that patients often stay longer than necessary in hospitals when insurance companies drag their asses and don't process work over weekends.

A day in a shitty hospital like that can cost anywhere from twelve hundred to four thousand dollars. Are you tired of hearing people talk about the ridiculous cost of healthcare? I am.

In this hospital, they began the initial steps of my recovery. They made sure I could drink fluids and eat safely. My nose hose that was running from my nostril to small intestine, nourishing my body during the long sleep, was removed. They initially capped my tracheostomy to make sure I could breathe on my own. Then, they removed my tracheostomy and performed painful wound care on the hole in my neck until it had mostly sealed itself over by around day three. The respiratory therapist named Freya, I think, sported a shield maiden's haircut and was the resident sadist performing this daily ritual. I thought she was going to kill me.

On a lighter note, I distinctly remember my swallow evaluation that determined if my naso-intestinal feeding tube was coming out. It sounds pretty basic, but in a critically ill patient, they have to make sure you can swallow normally for two reasons: ensuring nutrition and avoiding aspiration. Aspiration is when you literally inhale your food or stomach contents into your lungs. This can cause acute hypoxia, pneumonia, and even death as a result. Thus, the swallow evaluation is a big deal.

The speech therapist had me eat a bit of applesauce, drink something thick, and then drink some water. I passed with flying colors. Once I knew I had passed the evaluation, I pulled my feeding tube out myself.

It seemed like it was about a foot and a half long. As I was doing it, in slow motion I could see the speech therapist saying, "Nooooooooooooo!" as he clapped his hands to his cheeks. "Why the hell'd you do that?"

"I just really wanted that tube out," I replied.

From then on, I was known as "impulsive."

In my chart, they made it sound like I was impulsive as a result of my brain injury. I don't think it's impulsive to want a tube going from nose to esophagus to Hades out of your body. Plus, I've put many of those in. I know how they come out. Doctors make the worst patients, after all. Oh well. I was making big moves. Or at least I thought so.

I still was kind of flipping back and forth from reality to Vivid World at night, but the dreamscape adventures gradually became less real and less threatening. I was still on some pretty strong pain medications and mood stabilizers, to the extent I didn't remember a handful of FaceTimes with friends and colleagues.

Eleni says one of the best was when I talked to the chief resident on the urology service via FaceTime. She said I was pretty punchy while on my steady diet of drugs.

Apparently, I told the urology chief resident to go ahead and schedule some surgeries for me and that I would be back in two weeks. It's now been three or four months since we spoke. In addition, I'm told I reenacted the prison scene from *Midnight Express*, as a way of saying goodbye. Incidentally, I was wearing an eye patch while playing the part of Irene Miracle.

I had forgotten I was fitted with an eye patch for the persistent double vision I had from the stroke. For a long time, my eyes did not work in a coordinated manner to allow me to focus on any one specific object. I also could not read up close or read any small print such as text messages on my phone.

One of the most difficult aspects of this whole ordeal was that this happened at the height of the COVID-19 pandemic. I know with near certainty that if I had contracted COVID while on the ventilator for that long, I would not be alive today. A lot of people shared this concern, including the ICU charge nurse who prohibited all my resident and attending friends from coming by to see me. He wasn't popular after that, but it did probably reduce my chances of contracting the virus. And by extension, of dying.

Most unfortunately, my wife was not able to be at my side or make any decisions for me in person or learn directly of my progress or decline. She was at home tethered to a phone that wouldn't ring nearly enough, and she often did not receive much information on my course. Once I rejoined the living, not being able to see her was a stake through my heart. After some well-orchestrated groveling and genuine tears, my wife finagled her way in to see me at the intermediate hospital. She had been vaccinated and had a negative swab and thus was allowed to stay with me for about a week.

Having not seen my then-fiancée for a month, it was pure happiness to hold her close and kiss her. Yet, she tells me that, during that time, my affect was quite flat. I was previously a pretty animated guy who was quick to laugh, awkwardly smile, or become too quickly ill-tempered. A combination of the stroke, brain swelling, surgeries, and medications made me flat. To give an example, my wife showed me a cameo.com "cameo" that she and Jordan ordered for me from The Darkness frontman, Justin Hawkins.

First off, these badass Britons can really wail and are my favorite band bar none. His cameo was heartfelt and awesome, basically wishing me a successful recovery. All I could muster in response was "Man. That is cool."

She asked incredulously how excited I was to see this on a scale of one to ten. "Ten," I said, but I said it, apparently, like a heartless automaton. I was emotionless—save for some rationally inexplicable crying episodes—for several months. She did say, however, that the Progressive commercials about becoming your parents always made me grin like an insane person.

In the step-down hospital, there were two strictly polar types of employees: those that clearly hated their jobs intensely, and those that truly loved their jobs beyond measure. There were some damn fine people there that really took excellent care of me. There were others that probably didn't care if I died.

Due to the degree of my brain injury, I was not allowed to walk about the room or to the toilet by myself. In fact, I was too weak and uncoordinated to walk to the toilet. I was, however, able to urinate in a handheld plastic urinal, but given my poor aim, I was placed in a comically oversized diaper. Being down some 40 pounds in weight, I looked like a cross between the New Year's Baby and a prisoner of war.

The quantity of opiates I required for head pain in my recovery phase was moderate though, for unclear reasons, the inpatient doc had placed me on a lethal dose of stool softeners. My bowels paid a price. I would often get the sudden urge to defecate and require immediate assistance. If I wasn't attended to in time, which was often, I would quite literally shit the bed and require a change and a bed bath. This happened more than I'd like to admit.

I distinctly remember the stench of shit smelling like the disgusting meal I had force-fed myself the night before. During these helpless and embarrassing episodes, the ones who hated their jobs were prone to jostling me about, lifting me high up in the bed, and dropping me on my head, as if I had deliberately chosen to shit myself for my own entertainment. This hurt like a son-of-a-bitch and I would make it abundantly clear that they were hurting me. It didn't seem to make a difference. I was not accustomed to not being able to fight back. I wasn't a snitch either, so I wasn't going to get satisfaction either way.

Another thing that sent the ship awry was the fact that I could barely keep food down. My stomach had shriveled to the size of a racquetball, having not ingested solid food in roughly a month. Thus, when I tried to eat one of three square meals, it usually came right back up and onto the side of my bed and floor. They really started to hate me then. On the flip side, there were some fine folks at this place that rarely saw much appreciation for their devotion and who really did all they humanly could to ease my suffering and provide me a little dignity.

One in particular was a Venezuelan man named Antonio. In Venezuela, he had been an orthopedic surgeon for many years before his country imploded from hyperinflationary petroleum nationalization under the great Hugo Chavez. In America, however, Antonio was now demoted to a nurse, a large step down in terms of skill, status, and pay grade. This is like going from full-bird Colonel down to Private First Class overnight.

Coming from another country, he would not be able to be a specialized surgeon, and the credentialing alone would require several thousands of dollars and at least five years of being a sleepless subordinate. Not appealing to a guy in his fifties. Nor likely.

A lot of immigrants in healthcare have similar stories. After suffering a stroke, I would struggle constantly with the real possibility that I would face demotion or be flat-out fired. Thus, we had a good mutual understanding and an instant kinship.

My dad had called the hospital one day trying to get some answers. I still could not text or even answer my phone, I was in such bad shape. Antonio answered and gave him the scoop. A Spanish-speaker himself, my dad recognized his accent and told him to speak only Spanish to me, as it might be useful to my cognitive recovery. My real-life dad was a really smart guy.

From then on, it was Spanish-only between us. It was a bit of fun, a much-needed challenge, and it put me in higher regard with some of the other Spanish-speaking healthcare workers. If I had soiled myself or cried out in pain, Antonio was often there to tell me it was alright. "No te preocupas. You need help and I am here to help you," he'd say. I was not accustomed to needing or accepting help, but sometimes, I needed the reminders that doing so was okay.

21

DON'T GO TOWARD THE LIGHT!

After meeting the recovery milestones fairly quickly in the step-down hospital, I waited another four days for my insurance to coordinate my approval to go to greener pastures at the inpatient rehab hospital up the road.

I loathed that an army of non-doctor bureaucrats ultimately controlled my recovery in so many ways. In this purgatory, I spoke with many friends, old and new. As I said before, I was in a Denial Phase at this point and thus did not break down and cry it out with them over the phone, as some might have expected. Psychologically,

I was denying my new reality. Though even if I had wholeheartedly accepted it, self-reliance and stoicism would have kept me secure. Conversely, I liked being asked if I had seen "The Light" or talked to angels. Fortunately, I did *neither*, despite so many near-death experiences in the ICU.

One thing that really raised my hackles was how people would often give me the following two cents: "Ya know. You are gonna recover from this and get back to the way things were before. I know this because you have already survived the impossible and have been through so much." This really got my Irish up. In essence, they were saying that because I survived such a near-death, colossally unfortunate life event, returning to one hundred percent function would be a walk in the park.

These observations could not have been more inaccurate. I did not consciously make an effort not to die. I didn't see a light at the end of a celestial tunnel and do a U-turn before entering. I just simply did not die. I do not remember any near brushes with death. Unfortunately, only my loved ones experienced those, to their own heartfelt distress.

I was sedated for most all of it. Granted, I was by no means psyched about having brain surgery. Yet, I never expected death or made any plans for the unforeseen. I didn't really have many options if I wanted to live. It was not my own mettle that kept me from dying. It was mostly the hard work of the critical care and neurosurgical physicians and advanced providers who called the shots and made the tough decisions. They experienced more anguish in the moment than I did. I did not need to hear medical advice from non-physicians. But I suppose when you're in a state of denial, distress, and fear, it is easy to pick things apart. I appreciated their intentions, just not the advice.

"Having a physician die on your watch is fine if it ever happens," said no physician ever. That's anathema. That would be a complete nightmare and I don't know if I could emotionally recover if that had ever happened to me. Accordingly, a team of stressed-out physicians worked around the clock, to make sure I did not die.

Meanwhile, I was happily ending racism and killing old ladies in my mind. The only thing I had done to help myself not die was being healthy before the event that brought me to the hospital in the first place. I didn't smoke, and I ran at least twelve miles per week and lifted free weights at the gym. I found out later that a young general surgeon colleague had placed my tracheostomy tube. I have more respect for him than he will ever know. I've operated on physicians before. It's asshole-puckering. Physicians truly are the worst patients because they know exactly what you're doing to them and for some reason the universe likes for them to have more complications than the average human. Or so we like to think. We are karmic time bombs. Nonetheless, I knew he was sweating bullets cutting into my throat, and I respect him for his equanimity and drive to get the right thing done.

"If you can get through this, you can get through anything." A mere platitude. I can't stress enough how wrong it is to say such a thing to someone with a neurologic injury. I don't fault anyone for saying this. I know their hearts are in my corner. But all I hear is that because someone else lost a lot of sleep over you and used their years of training and expertise to save your life, you can now seamlessly get back to the way you were.

By the time I was over four months out from the injury, I had completed around eight weeks of intensive occupational, physical, and speech therapy, yet I had only made marginal gains. If I was sixty-five and nearing retirement, I would agree that I had made enormous gains over that time span. But I needed to get back to work and pay down school debt and a mortgage.

At that time, I could walk without a walker and my vision had improved quite a bit. But alas, at thirty-five years old, my left hand still moved like a trout with whirling disease, and I walked like an android. My thoughts went wild. I thought, just how the hell am I gonna get back to being a surgeon? Is it naïve to even think I will be? Will I be escorted off the premises at work like the stroked-out old vascular surgeon that practiced there when I was a resident? Will I go broke and default on my medical school debt? My mortgage? Have I lost key job skills just by the attrition of spending all my time in rehab?

"No, man," people would say to me. "You're gonna get through this because you're so young." Oh, okay. Wow. Thank you for that. I had almost forgotten that I was a young active adult that was brought to his knees by a freak stroke.

"You're so young" is another phrase that I continue to hear as well, even to this day. It's like nails on a chalkboard. I hear it from my non-medical and medical friends, my doctors. In theory, it is true. It is at least true of young, post-surgical patients who heal quicker than my older patients.

Regardless, it's a trite thing to say. What I hear is "Hey, because you have the superpower of being not greater than sixty-five, you are gonna make a quick and full recovery." The problem with this statement is that it displaces all the anguish and responsibility onto the person with the stroke.

It's like saying: "Look, you are thirty-five years old. This should be a walk in the park, even though I'm not qualified to say so. If you don't recover from this, it's because you didn't follow through and put in the work. I mean, you are thirty-five, aren't you?"

Yes, but I had a life of extremely high function. I cut on people, for God's sake. I would be golden if all I had left to do was retire and die. If only my recovery goals were making dinner and wiping my ass. But I got a lot of livin' left to do, chief. I don't even have children yet.

A therapist once told me that making a new connection in the brain to regain a skill takes about four hundred repetitions. Multiply that by about a million skills for which one needs their left arm and hand, and you have just south of half a billion repetitions—and this is under ideal circumstances.

22

ACT NATURAL

Humor me and imagine yourself on a long walk. I want you to ask yourself if your arms swing to and fro, especially when walking fast. The answer is YES, by the way. Now ask yourself if you consciously think about swinging your arms as you continue to walk quickly. It is certainly not something we think about, but it is something we quite unconsciously do. I used to, anyhow.

I am still working hard to try to make my gait look remotely natural and to let my arms swing as effortlessly as they once did. But alas . . . I'm a broken android. I'm trapped in a vessel of faulty wiring. People stare when I move. I don't blame them. It's incongruous to see a thirty-five-year-old, seemingly fit guy walk around like a drunken robot. It's sad to see, much less be.

"Act natural." This is nothing more than a paradox to a stroke patient. It's like saying be zen, but also pull yourself up by your bootstraps. It is harder than you think it would be. A lot harder. It's like asking a pubescent teen to smile. Or saying "Don't do it. Don't think about the color red." See what I mean? It's just more embarrassing for us with brain injuries when we attempt to "act natural." My left arm doesn't swing naturally to and fro. It flexes and jives every time I lose the least bit of concentration.

I joke (privately of course) with my urology colleagues that it takes about a year for most men to recover erections after a surgical prostate removal. And that's when we carefully dissect and sweep down the intact nerves and vessels tethered to each side of the gland. The tissue in my brain is not intact. A significant portion of it died, swelled, and was plucked from within my cranium. How will this improve in twelve months? Beats me. No one makes guarantees, and I am just a simple country urologist.

I called my wife towards the end of my stay at the step-down hospital. I was incredibly relieved to hear that my dog was okay and that my truck was in the driveway at home and not in a police impound in northern New Mexico. As I mentioned, the sedation dreams were so irrefragably real to me that my brain had some catching up to do.

23

GREENER PASTURES

After mentally treading water and languishing in the stepdown hospital for four more days, I finally got the approval to go to the inpatient rehab hospital. It was a Monday and the troops mobilized as if my transport was a military operation. Everyone reiterated the blueprint of my transport and spoke in soft voices for some reason. I was retested for COVID prior to my departure. Miraculously, I remained negative.

They weighed me, and as I mentioned earlier, I had lost forty-one pounds since my initial admission to the ICU. Two-aught-five to one-sixty-four. It was mostly due to muscle atrophy. I looked malnourished and was, to some degree. My wife, a thoughtful and

OCD-organizer, had brought me clothes, snacks, and therapy activities in a series of reusable grocery bags during my stay. A thousand-gallon duffel bag would have been more appropriate. I probably had enough supplies and clothing to climb Denali.

It was dusk when the transport guy arrived to drive me to the inpatient rehab facility. He was a nice Hispanic guy in his late thirties with a full head of hair gone gray.

I almost laughed when I saw them loading up what had to have been nine large grocery shopping bags full of my personal effects onto a trolley. They loaded me into a wheelchair and walked me down to the parking lot, where I was wheeled up a ramp and locked into the hollowed-out medical van.

We made the short journey to the rehab facility just as the sun was almost gone. I made it to a room with two beds and a bathroom, and I was elated to be its only occupant. After getting situated and feeling out my new caregivers, I fell into a deep sleep.

I no longer dreamed of nightmarish adventures. Instead, my dreams were pleasant ones and mostly of me having made a complete recovery. In this way, they were equally as believable as those from the Vivid World, though, instead of being a world-class fighter pilot or the front man for a glam rock group, I was a regular guy that walked with a normal gait from my car to a restaurant alongside my wife.

I was jogging in an Aspen glade. I was doing surgery again. I was like Bauby in the book *Le Scaphandre et le Papillon*, wandering through a vivid, neurologically intact world in my dreams. I temporarily escaped the limits of a broken body. Heretofore, I had taken things like walking from a parking lot to a restaurant for granted. However, in these dreams, it was as exhilarating as flying over mountains or shooting fire from my hands.

The following morning, I briefly believed I could walk again. I awoke early to the clamor of the nursing staff, whose lounge was adjacent to my ajar room door. They talked of eyebrow plucking and cosmetic tattoos. It got under my skin, as I had hit my call button to ask for water now fifteen minutes ago. They were ten feet away and couldn't be bothered. I was a "fall risk," and thus a pressure-sensing device was placed on my bed to alert the staff of me escaping.

I couldn't have escaped if I wanted to, I was so deconditioned. I did however hurl myself up to sitting on the edge of the bed, which set off a piercingly loud omnipresent alarm. That got their attention.

A tech came in, scolding me for setting off the alarm. It was silenced and I finally got my water. Just at the completion of a good long sip, a speech therapist came in. She didn't like the fact that I was drinking liquids in front of her without first being evaluated. Protocols, protocols!

After rationalizing my actions, she seemed no longer upset and repeated the same swallow evaluation I had performed eight days prior at the previous hospital. I was again cleared to eat and drink normal foods, though she pronounced the stipulation that my meats had to be chopped up by the food preparers. Fine by me. I remember my parents doing this for me when I was a child.

24

AWKWARD NUDITY

The next person to enter my room was an occupational therapist. In a snapshot, occupational therapists help you regain arm and hand strength and coordination so that you can bathe, use the toilet, brush your teeth, cook, and otherwise take care of yourself. Some also help with vision coordination and fine motor skills of the hands, to name a couple.

Her name was Brook. She was around twenty-five to thirty and was objectively attractive with a tall, fit build. As a new arrival, my first day was all about the initial evaluation. She needed to see how bad off I was from the stroke. Accordingly, she said today she needed to see how I shower and bathe myself.

Son of a bitch. This would be the last shred of dignity I could lose. She got me out of bed and wheeled me to the bathroom in the corner of the room. I felt like I was being led to slaughter. Why couldn't she have been a seventy-year-old, severely myopic grandparent?

She opened the door. In the small, brightly lit space, the square room was lined with grab rails. There was a toilet in the northwest corner and the shower head hung fastened to the tiled wall immediately in front of the toilet. You could sit on the toilet and touch the wall in front of you. Despite the shower head, it reminded me of the bathroom in my elementary school homeroom where my friends and I would play Bloody Mary.

The bathroom was frigid. Brook started the shower to get it warm and asked if I needed any help getting undressed. I lied and said, "No," rather emphatically. I awkwardly got into my birthday suit after laboriously pulling off my shirt and pants. I covered my genitals with a towel, though a washcloth would have sufficed. She helped me sit on the toilet, and the warm water jets from the shower pummeled my face and body. I wanted to immediately pee, but I held it out of embarrassment.

I could feel her eyes studying me as I ineffectively scrubbed my body with soap, mostly one-handed. I tilted my body to the right, hoping my emaciated trunk and thigh might obscure my penis from view. I hurriedly washed and rinsed the shampoo from my hair. Fortunately, after a point, she had seen all that she needed to see and moved herself behind a slightly agape bathroom door.

With the coast clear, I emptied my bladder into the toilet. She could not hear the forceful micturition over the loud shower, but I made sure to hurry it up. My urine was clear so there was no hurry to flush right away and blow my cover.

I let myself rinse a while longer then shut off the shower valve. I stood using the grab bar and waited. She helped me dry my body, but I was able to do about seventy percent of it myself. The fear of being naked in front of a stranger forced me to try and do more than I had been able to do previously.

At this point, I felt almost bad for her having to watch strangers bathe to evaluate their self-care shortcomings. This was a gritty part of the job but a crucial requirement, nonetheless. I got something like a "B" on that test and was allowed to go back to my bed after awkwardly slipping on a pair of boxers one-handed.

25

BRIAN

As I lay in bed watching television that day, I got a big surprise. A man around my age popped his head through the door about one minute before my physical therapy session was to begin. "Remember me?" I looked at him with uncertainty, as my vision was still a bit blurred. It was even more difficult to answer his question because his face was half covered with a mask and obscured by the light reflecting off his face shield. Then I replied, "Oh yeah!"

It was my friend Brian. We probably hadn't seen each other in at least five years, but back during my first two years of residency, he and I had often gone out for after-work beers at a local jaunt after the long hard days at the hospital. He had since gotten married, moved, and had a child. Sadly, I never got around to mooning him like I did the X-ray tech, coincidentally also named Brian.

It was so great to see a familiar face, but I was even more delighted when old-friend Brian told me he was going to be my physical therapist while in rehab. Physical therapists help mostly with movement, balance, and leg and core strengthening. I respected his breadth of knowledge regarding therapy and medicine when we used to pontificate over pints. But, five years had passed, and I knew he was now an experienced expert. He would soon prove he was. We got after it from day one.

After I was evaluated, he placed me in a thick nylon lederhosen with seat belt buckles sewn into the waistline. We then wheeled over to a large treadmill with a hoist device hanging about seven feet above the conveyer belt. I was buckled to the hoist. The hoist was lifted just to the point of testicle discomfort but not an inch more. This device essentially kept me upright and unable to fall over in any direction but, by design, didn't fully support my weight. Thus, the work of walking was still on me.

The treadmill started and I began walking on my own. Though shaky, this was the first time I had walked independently since crashing to my bedroom floor, and it felt good. I was "walking" with an asterisk, but nonetheless I was walking. I probably walked twelve hundred feet on that contraption my first time. This was about eight hundred feet farther than I had ever walked at one time since the stroke, and the previous times had been with a lot of assistance.

26

REBOOTING THE BRAIN

More than anything, Brian gave me quite a bit of ambition. He said I had great potential for major improvement as I was only thirty-five and had already been progressing quickly. Furthermore, he assured me he would get me out of this wheelchair soon enough and I would at least walk out of this joint with a walker. I'll be damned if he wasn't right about that one. Above all, it was nice to have a diligent, knowledgeable friend in my corner.

It might have been our first day together when he realized I had a more pressing issue that would be a huge hindrance to my therapy. My eyes. He could see them beating wildly with saccadic eye movements (rapid, and in my case, jerky eye movements), especially when looking from one side of the head to the other. "We need to get you to our neuro-ophthalmologist. She's great," he said. He explained that strokes, especially ones like mine, can cause serious changes to your vision and as a result can throw off your whole orientation.

He was right. My stroke made it so that the world I saw was on a new tilt. This made me more unsteady when trying to walk with the walker or the lederhosen grape smasher. I would come to understand later that my peripheral awareness had been affected by the stroke as well. This was due mostly to not being able to feasibly turn my head without a lot of pain due to the eight-inch incision through the back of my neck muscles and skull.

For over a month, I had either been sedated or looking straight ahead. I had little need to look about left and right, and if I did, it hurt like hell. Like atrophying muscles, your peripheral awareness is something you can lose if you do not use it. Other strokes can simply cause tunnel vision more directly by damaging the hardwiring. My issue, though, was the former, and until I underwent intensive therapy, I would be prone to getting winged by doorjambs and furniture. Or I guess it was me that was doing the "winging."

27

JEEPERS PEEPERS

I saw the neuro-ophthalmologist with Brian the following Thursday. She was as advertised. With a few deft exams, she knew the location of my injury, and I'm not even sure she read my chart. She didn't need to. The prescription was the following: various eye exercises, prism glasses during PT, and +1.00 readers like our parents have but can never seem to find. Jokes aside, the readers allowed me to read books and text messages, which was a huge win. They say a stroke automatically adds ten years to your vision. My dad told me he needed readers at forty, so that sounded about right to him.

Prism glasses are a different beast. They are specialized glasses that orient your visual horizon and tweak your mind's and body's visual perception so that you won't form bad habits that throw everything off. Though scientifically amazing, let me assure you they should never be worn in public.

Prism glasses feel like they are about a half-inch thick and look like they could burn the treads off a tank if you precisely focused the sun through them. They are large circles on a hefty frame and look like the glasses that Jerry Lewis wore when he offended most of the world portraying an Asian chef. But the undeniable truth was that they proved simply invaluable and worked wonders for my short road back to walking. An occupational therapist asked me the following day if the prism glasses worked. I said, "Of course they do. No one flirts with me anymore."

28

NEW ROOMIE

The following day I received the unsettling news that I would be getting a roommate. No one wants a roommate in the hospital. It multiplies the nursing disturbances by two, you have to share a bathroom, and you are forced to make small talk. I objected to this and was told by my treating physician that I would get a private room, but it never happened.

My new roomie had been recently admitted to the hospital and faced a hellacious hospital course similar to mine in many ways. We both had narrowly escaped becoming worm food. He got pneumonia from being on a ventilator and was currently receiving antibiotics in the rehab hospital through a PICC line in his arm. PICC stands for peripherally inserted central catheter. It is a long thin hollow tube that is placed at the bedside over a wire and runs from the inner arm to just above your heart. It is a safer way to administer long-term IV antibiotics, and he would be on them another few weeks in the hospital. I would get one much later in the game.

I told him I was a physician after a long introductory chat, and he asked me quite a few medical questions. I answered in such a way as to not give him the impression I was trying to be his new doctor.

He was morbidly obese, in his mid-fifties, and, from the history he provided, he had been admitted to the hospital for Pickwickian respiratory failure. In essence, his lifestyle had bought him a breathing tube along with some inevitable iatrogenic infections along the way. Pickwickian respiratory failure means that he was so fat he couldn't breathe well enough to oxygenate his body.

In this scenario, your breathing muscles simply don't have enough strength to lift the heavy fat apron off your rib cage, restricting lung expansion. Restricted lung expansion begets less oxygen intake. Less oxygen begets less energy production available to the muscles, such that they can't function properly. Such affected muscles include the respiratory muscles you require to breathe.

It's a spiral scenario. After a short chat, I sized up my oversized roommate. In contrast, his "brush" with death was completely preventable. If he had cut out soft drinks a year ago, he probably could have averted this situation. Honestly, I have little sympathy for able-bodied people of sound mind and four limbs that choose to put themselves in such a state of disorder.

But moving on, we had two separate miniature TVs almost side-by-side on our dressers. After dinner, we were largely civil regarding which television channel we would ultimately watch, so that for example *Ancient Alien Truckers* would not be playing over *Nude and Scared Shitless*. I thought to myself, "This may not be so bad. He's a nice enough guy."

Wrong.

His incessant snoring sounded like a sperm whale being fed tail-first into a wood chipper. My blood boiled and I paged the nurse pleading for a sedative and some earplugs. I said, "Are you not hearing this bullshit?" She had neither sleep aid to give me, and I passed the night awake and wishing for my release from this hell.

After keenly listening to his breathing patterns and watching him sleep for a short period, I diagnosed him with obstructive sleep apnea (OSA) and informed him of my findings in the morning. He said that yes, in fact, he had been recently diagnosed with this before his hospital admission. He did have a sleep study performed, so I asked, "Where's your CPAP?"

He admitted to having a CPAP but gave me some excuse about why he never used it. Perhaps the loving human in me had died, or at least retreated, but not the physician. I said, "Look, man. You have to wear that damned thing, like it or not. If you wanna go blind, have a heart attack, have a stroke, or have erectile dysfunction, then by all means don't wear it." That got his attention.

Men don't really care about an ounce of medical prevention when you warn of a pound of death. But bring up losing their erections, and you can get them to do anything—even take care of themselves. I wasn't lying about erectile dysfunction and OSA. It can also make men pee a lot at night. Look it up.

29

EYES ON THE PRIZE

I tried to stay positive and block out Captain Corpulence from my world. I had a job to do. I was here to will myself back into being a functioning human being. What anger and annoyance I endured the night before was shoveled into the boiler of my being. I hit therapy with lion intensity. I was seeing three types of therapists: physical, occupational, and speech. Given my speech was not affected, I spent most of my time with PT and OT. Speech was mostly there to help me polish up my cognition, which was dampened from brain swelling and surgeries.

Contrary to what one might think, the OT and PT sessions have always directly involved more work on my mind than any brain-busting memory or logic problem thrown at me by speech therapy. Even though you might think of these two disciplines as purely muscular in nature, they do require a laser focus that nearly overheats the brain.

You are asked to complete specific exercises that approximate some common natural movement or technique that will ultimately confer a small part of your rehabilitation. Yet, your body doesn't do it because your circuits were fried or cut out. You cannot do it. But you have to if you want to get back to the things you loved doing.

Your thinking self begins to panic. You're revving the engine with the pedal to the floor, but the clutch is still in first gear. You have been told by every impassioned therapist that the brain is an amazing thing, and they all have a story of Methuselah returning to rollerblading at six months after his stroke that was worse than mine.

So, you ask of yourself the impossible. You say, *Look, you son of a bitch. We are going to do this if it kills us both.* And you make something happen. The first few times you look like an absolute fool. You stumble. You literally drop the ball. You are failing but at least you are doing it in style.

Then, after lots of failing, you begin to start succeeding. You accomplish the impossible. Your soul, your being, your "amazing brain" just won a battle that puts you that much closer to winning the war. This parallels life lessons we've been fed our whole lives. Never give up. If at first, you don't succeed . . . I'll be damned. Could these tired clichés possibly be true?

I often think if I had not had this stroke and had applied half this level of focus to learning to play the piano or learning Icelandic, I might have been a contender for the most interesting man in the world. Repetition and iron will. That's what moves the needle.

After doing this daily for a few weeks, I was making big strides. The mostly sixty-five-and-up crowd of stroke patients in the therapy gym went from looking at me strangely to cheering me on. Brian and I were walking without a walker and doing some very light boxing-style training.

My insurance had told us it was time for me to leave the farm and I was ready to be home with my fiancée.

By this time, I hadn't been home in about two months. Eleni and I planned to get married at our home about twelve days after my return. I know. Lame, but the coronavirus pandemic forced us to do something quite small. Or, "intimate" as the vernacular now goes.

My wife-to-be planned to accompany me to Dallas for intensive rehab, but her employer could not legally give her leave without FMLA (Family and Medical Leave Act) approval. In order to qualify, we had to be married. So, our timeline got moved up a bit. I had already proposed. If we needed to get married a little sooner, so be it.

30

THE GREATEST ESCAPE

I knew I was nowhere near back to normal, but I was ready to be out of hospitals. Fifty-two days of hospital life is fifty-two days too many. I was tired of having to ask permission to leave my bed; tired of getting poked with needles in the middle of the night; tired of brushing my teeth in a bathroom stunk up by the ogre who slept next to me. I craved privacy, intimacy, and many specific foods. Prior to my departure, logistical arrangements were made. I was to be collected around 3:00 p.m. on a Sunday.

My wife was working that day. Due to the COVID surge at

that time, she had been transferred from the clinic to the hospital inpatient COVID unit. She was caring for the critically ill and even having to pronounce dead some young people near my age, killed by the virus. My wife is stronger than I'll ever be. After what she went through with me, she was seeing what could have been, every single day on the job. Thus devoted to her critical responsibilities, our friends Trevor and Jordan stepped up to the plate and came to pick me up.

When they arrived, my nine, conveniently reusable cloth Whole Foods grocery bags full of clothes and electronics were trolleyed up to their car. I busted out hot, in a walker, as I was not yet steady on long distances or uneven surfaces. Once we had all gotten reacquainted and situated in the car, I asked them if we could go get ice cream. I told them it was crucial to my recovery. They agreed, and we made our way to a bougie food court in Albuquerque that was part of a multi-tenant retail gallery. They had the best nitro creamery in the state, as far as I knew.

The place was packed, and after Trevor dropped us at the sidewalk, he parked the car and met us inside. I ordered a waffle cone with scoops of red chile chocolate and caramel-something Himalayan sea salt. They warned me that it would be extremely messy, and they recommended a bowl in lieu of the cone. I said, "Not today. Give it to me in a cone." I wondered if they didn't trust me to eat this ice cream cone because I was disabled or because it was messy.

We walked to our table outside and I felt the weight of a hundred staring faces. Nearby, an entire table of probably six people sat together, their eyes fixated on me walking with a walker. As I passed their table I stopped and said, "Be thankful for your health and what you have." They sort of half-receded and half-nodded as I walked away slowly like a curmudgeon.

When we finally sat down at the outdoor table, Jordan and Trevor just about lost it. They were giggling and kicking their feet asking me to tell them verbatim what I said to that table. I began to eat my ice cream like a ravenous dog starved of food, people, and love. I soon realized the girls at the ice cream counter were right about the bowl. I was getting melted ice cream and caramel on my cheeks, hands, my fleece, and pants. I was a mess and Jordan brought me a brick of napkins as she and Trevor cackled at my ice cream obstinacy. I didn't care how idiotic I looked. It felt good to eat ice cream on the outside on my own terms.

31

A JOYOUS HOMECOMING

My handlers eventually got me home, where they made arrangements for a reunion with my dog Indi on the back porch, to avoid a pee puddle in the house. I was beyond excited to see her. Just a short time earlier, I thought she was dead, lying cold and stiff somewhere in some mysterious region of Vivid World. Rattling through the front door in my walker, I proceeded awkwardly through the house to the back porch deck, where Indi immediately began vacillating between hardly recognizing me and unbridled excitement. She couldn't quite figure me out at first; she was scared, I think, by the large walker and my shaved head.

There was no loss of urine and no excessive licking as I'd expected. Just uncertainty and a little love here and there, as if she sensed, in her own way, that I was wounded. Before long, however, I would fall back into her herd as the alpha dog, but for a few days, I was the Manchurian Candidate to her. Being the occasion of my "triumphant" return home, my wife left work a bit early that day and got home soon after we arrived. It was so unreal seeing her again at home. She was so incredibly radiant. I told her how beautiful she was and she of course told me that wasn't true because she just got off work. I hugged her tightly and gave her the biggest kiss I could, and for a split second, it felt like everything was back to normal.

I felt like I had just won the Super Bowl. Accordingly, Trevor, or perhaps it was Jordan, asked me what I wanted to do next. I wanted to say, "I'd like to jog two miles without falling," but instead I said, "I wanna drink a beer." They poured me a fancy craft lager into a cold mug, and I took a big swig. "Ughhh, this tastes like shit," I said. It tasted like that first hot beer I struggled to get down in the ninth grade in Will Harper's attic. We paid a high school senior thirty dollars for twenty-three room-temperature Keystone Lights. What a deal.

Prior to the stroke, I, like Ben Franklin, thought that beer was proof of the Divine. Now I couldn't finish a pint. Because in fifty-two days, I'd lost that acquired taste I had worked so hard to develop in college, though it was almost a nostalgic experience to get to relive my first beer. Things tasted much differently after almost two months of eating or being tube-fed hospital nutrition, and it wasn't just beer.

It was like I had just come off the space travel diet. My stomach didn't know what to think. While I was in the step-down facility and the rehab hospital, a few fine friends snuck me up some meals from some of my favorite local restaurants. But it was hard for me to finish them. Sometimes I would finish a wonderful dish only to bring it right back up minutes later onto the hospital floor. The meals tasted like they were loaded with sodium. I'm sure they were, but after a month-long palate cleansing, it was like I could keenly taste all the individual components and their concentrations. Kind of how I imagine dogs taste things.

It really made me think. I'm sure restaurant chefs intentionally, or perhaps even unconsciously, bring the amounts of butter and salt in their dishes right up to the threshold between good and too much, in order to addict our caveman brains to their high-octane fuel.

I recalled the days when I worked for a restaurant tycoon in West Texas. He had four heart attacks and at least that many ex-wives. I asked him once what the secret to his success was. He said, "Butter." I think that rounds out my point.

In a sense, I had been disconnected from the "Matrix." If one good thing came out of that ordeal, it was that I had a chance at clean livin'. I'm now growing my own tofu and I eat kale burgers every Monday. Right. I'm not a monk! And besides, who wants to live to forty?

It took some adjusting, but after a few weeks I went back to regular meals. It's not like I really ever ate much fast food anyway. My wife is Greek, and I was once a self-sufficient bachelor, so there aren't any shortages of cooks in the kitchen.

32

MY LOVELY WIFE

The following week alone with my wife was fantastic. It didn't seem real. I felt such an appreciation for privacy and not being pestered constantly. To be able to hold her and kiss her felt like one of my sedation dreams, and a privilege I didn't deserve. She had the week off as she was doing week-on, week-off hospital shifts in the COVID units. We had gotten engaged and agreed to eventually cohabitate at my house about two weeks before my stroke.

In my absence, my wife had turned our house into a home. A home straight out of a West Elm catalogue. I had vague hospital memories of her half-asking for permission to redecorate, but

I didn't care. I just wanted her to do things that made her happy and things that might take her mind off the stress and hardship my issues were certainly causing her.

The home looked respectable and exceptional. She painted walls, hung wallpaper, and filled just about every room with enough plants to offset a percent of human civilization's carbon emissions.

It's a miracle if I don't get whacked by at least two plants in the morning when I get up to make coffee. She is an organizational nut with a great sense of color and interior design. I'm a disorganized basket case who thinks interior decoration is buying a leather couch. So, we complement each other well.

Despite our West Elm meets Amazon rainforest décor, my wife also rigorously followed the occupational therapists' advice to essentially kid-proof the house for me. She and our friends put up grab bars on my shower and toilet, they removed a rug from under a four-hundred-pound coffee table and put in a shower chair. Two of the guys even took a break to hang my knock-off samurai sword up on a wall in my office. That was special.

With the exception of the sword, I have outgrown most of these ergonomic adaptations, but I still use the shower grab bar and I think about the person who installed it every time I need it. Thus, if you ever ask yourself what you can do for someone who's had a stroke, do something like that. It means a hell of a lot more than dropping off a fruit basket. But, one extra piece of advice: go straight to asking their spouse. If you ask the stroke patient, he will tell you he doesn't need anything done to his house.

A small group of friends had participated in a meal train such that we had dinner provided Monday, Wednesday, and Friday. In other words, each person or couple brought us dinner on their assigned day. Some cooked and others brought us food from our favorite restaurants. It was a much-appreciated gesture and was a pleasant excuse to see friends during COVID lockdown. This was a great gift idea. I know my wife was most appreciative.

33

THE PRODIGAL PARENTS RETURN

The following week, my parents came to stay with us to provide some caregiver relief for Eleni, who had to return to hospital work. Our reunion was not like any other. I love my parents, but as the youngest child, I have always been more of a lone wolf.

Due to COVID, my parents had not been permitted to come visit me in the hospital. Still, there wasn't much they could do while I was sequestered anyway. They were kept abreast of my hospital course. Yet, I know the information was patchy at times, and having to receive bad news over the phone, I'm certain, was hard on them.

Even if my room had been mic'ed with a direct feed to my parents' phones, so much would have been lost in nonverbal communication.

Thus, when they got out of my dad's truck, I could see their faces go from concerned to relieved. They knew I was at home and out of the hospital, but it was like they had to see it for themselves to believe it. Our hugs were longer than normal. It felt strange not being able to offer to unload their luggage.

Once they got settled in, my mom started dinner while we snacked on a bag of homemade cookies. They regaled us with all the hometown gossip and current events, as if things were status quo, and their son had not, just recently, nearly died. Normally, hearing the San Angelo obituaries secondhand, or the "news" of a new chain store opening in my hometown, would have irked me, but I was just happy they were there.

We were having steaks, a salad, and risotto. They had heard how much weight I lost and therefore a big steak was the prescription. My dad, a cattle-trading cowboy with a rapier wit, believes there is little a big juicy steak can't cure. Other than heart disease, I would have to agree.

From the beginning of the dinner plans, I demanded to make the risotto. I wanted to show off the rehabilitative progress I had made in such a short period. I grabbed an onion and a cutting board and positioned the onion under my bizarrely postured left hand.

I started to make the first cut when I realized the large chef-knife was grazing my left index finger. "Nope, not ready for this," I said. Eleni, watching me like a friendly hawk, stepped in and diced the onion for me. At this point, I was solely reliant on my right hand. Once I had the requisite ingredients, I was able to stir in wine and broth, doing my share of the dinner preparation.

I reluctantly delegated the steak grilling duties to my dad. I wasn't about to multitask. Once dinner was prepared and the red wine was uncorked, we sat down for a feast. I was anemic and craved red meat. Eleni had to cut my steak as I wasn't yet able to do it.

While I attacked the meat in front of me, Eleni had a carrot cake baking in the oven that almost picked me up out of my chair like a cartoon scent trail. In anticipation of the cake I made sure to save some room in my hospital-shrunken stomach. After dinner, the cake was iced, cut, and placed on small, handmade ceramic plates that my wife had bought in Asheville, North Carolina.

I grabbed two plates and began the short walk to the table to begin serving. I didn't get two feet before my left hand, acting on its own accord, jettisoned the plate and cake slice into the sink, shattering the plate to bits. The poor slice of carrot cake was lying face down in a bowl of dirty dishwater. "Goddammit, you fucking retard!" I yelled loudly at myself.

I was visibly upset. A fumarole atop a sleeping volcano of simmering anger had erupted, exposing what lay beneath. "Don't worry about it. Plates are replaceable," they all said. I told myself, so are people. So are jobs. So are urologists. I hadn't just broken an expensive plate. I had broken a relentless momentum heretofore free of worry and future-casting.

34

THE FEARS OF A RUMINATING MAMMAL

But now I ruminated about my future, my career, my medical school debt, my car loan, and the potential to support my family. Thank God we had no children at this point. This was the first time I had even thought of such things since my stroke. Living in the moment is pretty easy in a hospital. You never really feel the need to look beyond your next meal or your next surgical procedure.

The real world's not so predictable, nor reliable, and thus mindfulness is a billion-dollar industry. I finally reined myself in and feigned equanimity. I got another piece of cake and carried it to the table, this time with my right hand. We awkwardly finished dessert and I left the table to take my evening medications.

I felt conflicted. I was torn between hating myself for losing my temper and liking myself for expressing my true emotions in front of my family. In either scenario, it didn't feel right. I know they are capable of imagining what I am going through, but they don't really know. Of course they can't. And to expect them to is presumptuous on my part.

My dad, however, knows better than most. He was in a terrible accident while on horseback in 1999 that almost took his life. The specifics remain unclear, but, in summary, a green colt ran him through several mesquite trees, breaking both his arms and one leg. The horse stopped from a dead sprint and hurled him face-first into a fence post like a rag doll. He was beat to hell and bleeding, but somehow managed to walk about a mile to the tack room. He only remembers struggling to pick up the phone to try to call 9-1-1, but his arms were broken, and his hands were too slick from blood to pick up the phone. He then passed out, probably from blood loss. By sheer happenstance, my granddad returned to the tack room office out of boredom. That's where he found his son, lying there on the tack room floor in the throes of death. Not chancing on calling 9-1-1 and waiting for an ambulance, he drove him to the hospital himself, in time to save his life. Makes you wonder if impatience isn't somehow virtuous after all.

I apparently forgot this saga during my tantrum. He was in the hospital a similar duration to mine, and I remember my mom having to wipe his ass for a month while his arms were still broken. He's more of a workaholic than I am. I know it killed him to be out of commission that long. But then, bones heal, after all.

Does a brain that's been cut on? I hear a lot of positives and stories of hope from friends, family, and therapists, but nothing is concrete enough to hang my hat on. I initially made big gains, but not enough to return to my job and calling. Presently, I'm riding a long miserable plateau.

Many of my therapists and much of what I've read corroborate that stroke recovery is nonlinear. It's a staircase, and after summiting a riser, there can be long periods where you remain standing on one of the treads. Though tedious and highly annoying, I have found this to be true. There was a mountain to climb from the get-go. I pleaded with my battered brain to work hard with as much mindfully directed intention possible to, say, learn to walk again without a walker. The mountain climb was slow, but I was at least facing and traveling upward.

Once I had reached the top, it was no longer a mountain, but a vast desert mesa with no landmarks in any quadrant. Now it was like I was directionless, with no estimation of how long it would take me to reach the next summit to be climbed. That is the frustrating part when it comes to brain injuries.

I had heard this concept before, but I chose not to believe it or dwell on it. I am thirty-five years old. Most of what is known and described in the literature with respect to stroke patients has got to be heavily based on the outcomes of elderly individuals, or so I reasoned. That's the group that gets the most strokes. How would their successes and failures apply to me? I'm an old soul, but I still have a young body.

35

BACK TO SCHOOL

I awoke the next morning and got ready for another treacherous shower. At this point, showering was still a bit precarious. I continued to have issues with balance, and my left leg, without its normal brain-guidance, tended to heel-strike the tile floor like a jackhammer. This had created bruising in my calcaneus bone that remained painful for several weeks after.

Regardless, I got the job done and readied myself for a field trip to outpatient physical therapy: day one. My mother, my interim handler, drove me to the physical therapy facility. It was like being driven to middle school all over again! Her coonhound mutt, Duke, came with us to look out the window and go for a walk while I did therapy. Duke is a wise and gentle dog who I always wished was mine.

I met with the therapist, whom I could tell was used to seeing primarily sixty- to eighty-year-old patients that had just received a new prosthetic hip or knee. He didn't seem thrilled to see a young doctor with a stroke.

I had heard that over the past decade or so, physical therapy had diverged into two disciplines within itself, composed of stroke rehabists and orthopedic rehabists (who mostly take care of patients with newly placed prosthetic hips and knees). More or less, rehabbing people with a hip or knee replacement is essentially the same for each patient. The hardware really doesn't change, nor does the physics.

Strokes, however, are so varied in location and presentation that each patient is unique, with myriad problems to address. Thus, therapists typically have to spend more time with stroke patients than say a cat lady with a new hip. Therefore, it's more economically advantageous to focus one's practice on the orthopedic stuff. It definitely generates the most income.

So, in a fledgling pseudo-metropolis like Albuquerque, there really aren't a lot of neuro-specific physical therapists to be found. This was only a temporary bridge anyway. In two weeks, I would be in Dallas, going to an intensive stroke rehab program and living temporarily with extended family. Nonetheless, I did what was asked of me, and I indeed learned some new exercises to take away as homework.

For the remainder of the week, I would do my daily physical therapy routine and walk thirty minutes on the treadmill, using the rails to keep me upright and moving in place. My mom and I played at least ten games of Rummikub every day, as that activity was good for my visual tracking and attention.

36

RESTORED TO DEFAULT SETTINGS

My attention issues from the stroke were like a pile of dug-up bones. I like to think of myself as a recovering attention-deficit addict. When I was a kid, I had just about the worst Attention Deficit Disorder you could have.

I remember reading the DSM-IV criteria on ADD in medical school and laughing out loud in the library. As a child, it was common for me to completely forget what I was doing right in the middle of actually doing that something. I could never complete a series of assigned tasks at one time, as I'd never remember or care what the second task was.

Historically speaking, for me this occurred around the time that ADD was becoming an in-vogue diagnosis, but I don't think my parents were familiar with the disorder. I'm pretty sure they had me IQ-tested in lieu of seeing a professional because, from the outside, I probably seemed pretty dumb.

I know my attention problems were annoying and costly to my parents. I would often leave the water hose running or leave my new basketball shoes in the gym to be stolen. I paid the price often and would get spanked and berated, mostly by my mother, for my apparent forgetfulness.

So, for about the next eight years from childhood through high school, I would write everything down that I had to or wanted to complete that day. I was like a mini-Guy Pearce in *Memento*, though it never came to tattoos. Notepads were fine. I seemed to finally kick the habit of poorly sustained attention and went on to score very well in medical school and on medical standardized tests.

After the stroke, it was like my brain reset to default mode, and I've been struggling ever since with getting my attention back to where it was. I'm back to writing notes and "to-do" lists, but given that I'm trying to get back to work, I've become extra hard on myself when I do something "ADD."

It's peculiar how after you have had a stroke, you are judged on a new rubric. There's no room for error. If you walk funny or forget to do something, you are presumed to be deficient because of your stroke, not because of some propensity predating it. It's like having your second beer at a party and dropping it on the kitchen floor purely by accident, say because you're just a klutz, thus causing everyone to glare at you like you're already wasted. You want to say something, but it's pointless and may only make things worse.

Prior to my stroke, I enjoyed being a man apart. I was beholden only to my patients and loved ones, some of whom may or may not have known about any tics or quirks I might have always had. And they accepted them for what they are. Nowadays, it seems I can't stay away from judgment's microscope.

In trying to get back to work and simply do the mental and cognitive portions of the profession, like the clinical side for example, it often seems as though my employer overlords view my physical limitations as a direct reflection of my ability—or inability—to think critically and make decisions. It sometimes feels like I'm at the end of my rope career-wise.

When you're at the end of your rope, I know you're supposed to tie a knot and hang on for dear life. But sometimes, you'd rather tie a noose. Or, maybe you're just supposed to tie a knot and swing to another tree.

37

FIRST COMES LOVE

After my parents left, Eleni and I had the remainder of the week to pack for our trip. The plan was to drive to Dallas and stay with family while I participated in an intensive stroke rehab program. But first, we drove up to Santa Fe to get our marriage license in advance of our small wedding at the house. It was eerie seeing the usually busy and bustling streets of Santa Fe devoid of industrious locals and meandering tourists.

That Saturday was our wedding day. Jordan got licensed to marry people on the internet and was our officiant. Trevor helped get a tie and cuff links on me before the wedding started, but I could mostly do everything else.

There were about ten attendees, consisting of close friends living in Albuquerque. Not many more could or would come due to COVID. Eleni had bought us cheap silicone wedding bands for the ceremony. Even for this intimate, small-scale ceremony at home, Eleni had put the event together as if she were a professional wedding planner.

Bouquets of roses, eucalyptus, and blue thistles were placed on every elevated flat surface in the house and back patio. My little rank cow dog was wearing a white bandana around her neck that read "My Humans Are Getting Married." Lanterns were lit with tea candles and placed on the flat railing surrounding the deck. They looked like luminarias.

I lit a small fire in the chimenea for warmth and ambience. We had coolers full of beer, bottles of wine, and five-gallon glass cooler dispensers full of iced tea and water. Eleni had made a ton of pasta with a tomato meat sauce and a bunch of salad before getting ready for the ceremony. I met the photographer and her husband.

With everyone present, I was positioned on the deck next to Jordan with Trevor at my side. Everyone took their seats on the outdoor furniture and the wedding began. I stood there with my flat stroke affect and waited.

I thought to myself how lucky I was to have such a beautiful, caring, and committed partner in life. Had it not been for her, I'm not certain I would have survived this terrible life event. What I do know for certain is that my recovery would not have been as successful as it is presently. She truly made sacrifices and endured a great deal of pain just to continue being with me.

I've heard of such dedication and acts of love through my patients, though I never had a reason to experience it myself. Had she not made these sacrifices and further pushed me to recover, I would not have attended an intensive stroke rehab program in another state. Sure, I could have braved COVID and flown to Dallas on my own, or I could have convinced my parents to take me there. I could have bribed a friend. But I don't know that I would have had the fundamental discipline to go it alone, to make myself go through that just to be a little bit better.

Were it solely up to me, I probably would not have gotten past looking into it. I would have rationalized that I couldn't afford it, or that I'd made enough progress in such a relatively short time that I didn't need specialized therapy in a city ten hours away from home.

I knew people like her were few and far between, and I was effusively happy and in love with her. I was ready to be married. I was glad we were not postponing our lives because of an onerous yet tragic pandemic. Yet I worried that my lack of giddy tearfulness would make me appear callous or unmoved by this solemn joining of our lives. My affect was still mostly flat from the stroke. Furthermore, I had been married before and knew what to expect as a primary participant in the wedding.

The one thing I took from that previous experience was to make myself be consciously in the moment and try to remember every nuance of the event, because it flies by in the blink of an eye. I told myself to be a walking camera and to make and store these memories. It didn't matter. All the self-coaching in the world could not have prevented so sublime an experience from flying by in a blink of mirth and pure happiness.

I stood there by Jordan's side and everything got quiet. The high desert air was crisp and dry. There was no wind. My bride came walking through the back door dressed in a dazzling white dress. She was wearing blue high heels and a white furry vest that reminded me of a baby bird's down coat. I was waiting for her to sprout glorious wings from the down and fly away to join the Seraphim. She was wearing red lipstick and was smiling ear to ear.

When she appeared, I said, "Holy shit! This is a real wedding!" Jordan giggled. It was as if seeing Eleni, looking so lovely and serene, simply eroded away my stone face and put me smack-dab in the moment. When she approached, Jordan hugged her, then I hugged and kissed her. Jordan began the ceremony:

> *. . . Today is an important one, because you are making a promise to one another that, in so many ways, you have already lived out. To stand tall, in joy and in pain, and to show up for the one you love. Today, you make the promise to continue forward as the family you've already proven yourselves to be.*
>
> *I'd like to share a quote with you all from* The Road *by Cormac McCarthy, a postapocalyptic novel full of hardship and terror. In such a bleak state, the narrator sheds a profound light into the value of togetherness.*

> "*Lying under such myriad stars. The sea's black horizon. He rose and walked out and stood barefoot in the sand and watched the pale surf appear all down the shore and roll and crash and darken again. When he went back to the fire he knelt and smoothed her hair as she slept and he said if he were God he would have made the world just so* and *no different.*"

I imagined myself to be the narrator in this last bit of the quote. I admit I wish I never had a stroke.

I think, *Would I be willing to go back in time in order to have not had this stroke?* What if the only way to have avoided it was to send me back to the beginning of residency, or even the beginning of college? Or even further back? Would I do it? I have mulled this hypothetical over time and time again, and I think, *No*.

I'm not an expert in the Butterfly Effect, but I worry (needlessly of course) that in an alternate timeline, I may have never met the love of my life. She's too important to me, and I wouldn't play God if it meant I might lose her.

We stated our Declarations of Intent and exchanged silicone rings. We kissed and were now happily married. The woman I had met in World War II, with whom I'd hatched premature babies from clay, was now my wife.

We took about a hundred pictures, cut the cake, and all sat down for an outdoor dinner on a banquet-sized foldout table large enough for the entire wedding party plus all of our guests. When I look back at the pictures from the wedding, I'm stunned by how swollen the back of my head and upper neck were. This area on my body was convex, though it should have been the opposite. In one picture, you could see clearly that the back of my head was completely shaved and revealed an enormous vertical scar still red from healing. I was embarrassed to some degree, but in the end, glad that there was photo-documentation of that cringeworthy scar.

38

HONEYMOON IN DFW?

We spent our last days at home in paradise and planned for our trip to Dallas for intensive rehab. Most couples go on honeymoons. We were no longer most couples.

We packed Eleni's car full to the brim and began our ten-hour drive to Dallas. We stopped several times in Texas to fill up on gas and snacks. It was clear Texas's COVID restrictions were much more lax than New Mexico's. Few people wore masks inside the cramped convenience stores. We were still quite rigid about mask-wearing, given my current state of health and vulnerability.

At one point, we approached a small gas station about four hours from Dallas. It was cold and windier than hell. While filling up, we went inside the small convenience store for some Dr Peppers and snacks. This time the place was empty; there was no one inside except for an amicable cashier who was interested in our journey. She told us that the winds were expected to reach thirty miles-per-hour and the temperature would drop to six degrees Fahrenheit by 2:00 a.m. I believed her.

We checked the weather on our phones. It looked like the whole state of Texas was about to be immersed in bone-chilling cold and blowing snow. We hustled onward to Dallas while night was beginning to fall. The wind was howling, and the bare trees swayed in the gusts.

My wife put on her music on a random shuffle and I was soon reminded of her undying love for the Backstreet Boys. She and her sister had made a music video honoring the musical harmony group when they were kids. I tested the strength of her professed fandom. "Can you name all five members of the Backstreet Boys?" She said, "AJ, Nick, Brian, Kevin, and uhhhh . . ." I goaded her for the fifth member's name. She punched me and I asked if the "Nick" she was referring to was "Nick Lachey." She said tersely, sounding offended, "Of course not. He was 98 Degrees." Like I knew. "Is it 'tearing up your heart' that you can't think of the last member of Backstreet Boys, Eleni?" Annoyed, she said, "That's NSYNC." I was batting a thousand with the boy band trivia.

I googled the group and told her it was Howie. She was relieved but still visibly irritated. For my blatant transgression, I was forced to listen to Backstreet Boys for the remainder of the drive.

Honeymoon in DFW?

A few songs in, we were passing Denton. I asked her if she'd heard of the band the Toadies. She said no, and acknowledged, as if in surrender, that I was the pop culture expert of our little duo. Clearly.

"Did the Backstreet Boys go to UNT?"

"Oh, honey. They didn't go to college," she replied with professorial certainty. I laughed.

39

GETTING TO WORK

We made it to the greater Dallas area, which is a common thing to say, but also one of the vaguest things you could say. Dallas is more a region in Texas than a city. We drove to a suburb where her sister and brother-in-law lived with their brand-new baby girl. They had made up the guest bedroom for us.

We arrived in one piece around 8:00 p.m. Nic and Seraphina helped us carry up our bags. I was still plugging along with a walker at this point and was little help. I felt ashamed. We ordered in Thai food and had some laughs over beers. That night, I took every sleep aid in my possession, as I knew I was a poor sleeper in new environments. As if to make sleeping any harder, the wind howled throughout the night, and it snowed full tilt like it would never stop. We could feel the cold creeping in with all the trappings of a major storm.

The next morning was something else. Nic and Seraphina were up early feeding the baby and the news on TV was squawking about the storm of the century. There were power outages all over the "greater" Dallas area. It was well below freezing outside, and the ground was covered in a billowing sea of snow.

Crushed snow on the streets was becoming one big ice rink with each vehicle that rolled over it. My wife and I bravely ventured off on the forty-minute drive to another Dallas suburb where the rehab facility was located. We made it to the I-40 toll road, which was covered in ice and slushy snow. Eleni's hands were white-knuckled on the steering wheel, her eyes intensely focused on the road as she navigated among a caravan of seemingly more timid drivers. It took us about an hour and a half to make it to the rehab facility, but we made it without crashing. Eleni helped me truck across the frozen tundra with my walker, and on into the facility.

The first day consisted of initial evaluations. I was getting good at being initially evaluated. After the decorum ceremony with my wife and the lead counselor—and an hour of teaching people how to spell my name—we got right to work. They did things a bit differently in Texas. Maybe it was because of tort reform.

The physical therapist had me walking on my own on day one. I asked if I should at least wear a gait belt. "No, I'll catch you." A gait belt is one of those thick cloth belts that have pink and blue pastel stitching running through them. It's what they make you wear in medical environments so they can grab you by your trunk if you start to fall. It's a handle for your handlers.

This was about the first time that someone had trusted me without any medically or rationally valid reason to do so. I was nervous as all hell, but I walked around like a foal taking its first steps. I was gazing around each room to see if there were any other brain-injured folks around my age, like a kid looking for new playmates. But there were none.

Eleni had told me this center was big on stroke rehab in younger patients trying to get back to work, but I saw no one within ten years of my age.

With the completion of morning therapy, my wife had long since left and it was time for lunch. Using my walker, I ambled to the cafeteria and sat down. With COVID still a threat, we were all seated at separate small tables, and there was a still silence in the large dining area. It was an unfamiliar and eerie environment. It was a room of solely brain-injured patients gazing straight ahead of themselves with thousand-yard stares, not saying a word. Some people, like myself, had large scars dressing their heads. Others just appeared blank, or seemingly sad. I felt like I had seen this before. *One Flew Over the Cuckoo's Nest* came to mind.

Granted, this was much more bizarre, but I wondered if this is what most kids nowadays are dealing with, in school districts where social distancing and other COVID restrictions are in place. My memory of a cafeteria was a place to eat with friends, of course, but also to socialize, cut up, and do pranks. In middle school, my friends and I would release wasps in the cafeteria, watch the world burn, then shoot soft drinks through our noses from laughing so hard. Now it was just a place of food consumption due to a socially confining virus.

I ate my hamburger and returned to more therapy for the remainder of the day. Eleni picked me up and told me the power was out at the house, and that we were driving to her parents' house in a nearer suburb to stay until the power kicked back on. That ended up taking three or four days, and even my therapy was canceled while we waited for a huge swath of the United States to warm up again. This unprecedented weather event became known as "Dallaska," or more broadly as "Snowpocalypse," and it put a major dent in Texas's energy hubris.

When life returned to normal, we did the same daily routine of driving to therapy, putting in the work, then driving back. To me, therapy was my new job and I treated it as such. I was always trying to push it, in the hopes that I could return to a normal life as quickly as possible.

Typically, in the afternoons at therapy, the last three hours were meant to be structured time for me to complete the homework from my morning lessons. I would usually hit the treadmill, do hand-eye-coordination exercises, and crank out logic puzzles.

It was a mind-body improvement camp. Every bit of it was necessary and useful towards achieving my end, even when I had to do activities with other members in the program.

There is one activity I'll never forget. If you've not played Pictionary with a gaggle of brain-injured adults, you're missing out. It was an absolute riot. If you're not familiar with the game, it basically works like this: A member of your team is given a randomly selected word and must try to "picture" the word (or what it represents) by drawing an image or images on a whiteboard. The object is for the other members to guess what the word is, judging from the drawing on the whiteboard. No talking or hints are allowed from the artist. The first member of my team, Bill, was up to bat. The opposing team already had five points on us. His word was "butterfly." He stepped up to the board, tremulous. He stood there staring at a blank board as the minute-long hourglass peed sand. He wouldn't draw.

We all shouted, "C'mon, Bill! Just draw something!"

He was visibly perplexed. "I, I, I, I, I . . . I can see the word," he said. "I just can't draw it."

Bill clearly had some form of expressive aphasia. Most often associated with spoken words, an expressive aphasia is when the brain has trouble producing language. At roughly second fifty, Bill drew two circles.

"Basketball!"

"Bowling ball!"

"Ant!" we each blurted out.

The minute was up, and we had zero points.

"Shake it off, Bill."

"That was a hard one," we lied.

A rudimentary drawing of a stick with wings would have been helpful.

The next member on the opposing team had "skateboard." Her team guessed it within seconds. She then told us the irony: "That's weird that I got this word. That's how I got my brain injury." She then explained that she tried getting on her son's skateboard, which immediately slipped out from under her feet, landing her on her head. This woman was nearing fifty, overweight, and had no business being on a skateboard.

The mood went from pitiable hilarity to instantly somber. The remainder of the session was much quieter, as at this point, we were just trying to be done with the game. The weeks went on. I was making some steady improvements, though I still had minimal function of my left hand. I had a long way to go to becoming a surgeon again.

40

PAINTING

Most nights, I found myself on Nic and Seraphina's back porch drinking light beer and painting. Painting quickly became a great outlet for me. It's something I can do mostly with my right hand. I was an artsy kid growing up, and I liked to draw and paint even back then. I enjoyed the meticulous nature of detailed acrylic brush paintings but later lost the bug. However, the rigors of medical study and the tedium of surgery seamlessly filled this void. I later discovered palette knife painting during the first COVID summer. Palette knife painting is exactly as it sounds: using different types of knife-like trowels to apply paint to canvas rather than brushes.

I liked that one could paint five hundred square inches in a mere few hours, and how it required more thought and planning than, say, painting a detailed picture of a dog. It was more about the journey than the destination, whereas a detailed painting or surgery was quite the opposite. I liked that you had to make your own map in your head before beginning. How to layer the painting. What textures to use. What colors contrast well with one another. Yet, I never seem to follow the maps to the letter, and that is the fun of it.

I do believe form follows structure, but not a hundred percent. Inspiration seems to follow deviation. It can be a deviation of whim or rebellion, but it is usually sparked from within. The mold, figuratively speaking, breaks from within. You can't break it if you aren't in it at some point. It otherwise wouldn't be "the mold." Most of my molds are homemade.

The best trips abroad I've taken started with a well-thought-out plan, but always diverged happily into something greater. Same goes for good paintings. The same goes for my career. If you had told me I'd be a human plumber in my first year of medical school, I'd have said you were going to be a psychiatrist, because you're crazy. A stroke was certainly not part of my plan, but I have no choice but to try to make something better of it. Painting is something I can still do despite the stroke and is more important to me now than ever before.

My sister-in-law's husband, Nic, saw my paintings on Instagram and wanted to try his hand at painting as well. I brought four or five gesso'ed canvases with me to Dallas. It was nice to have some artistic company and a drinking buddy.

I spent our first painting session trying to help Nic paint a large mountain jutting into an ocean bay in an abstract, palette knife fashion. I showed him everything I had learned through trial and error, YouTube, and reading. It actually turned out pretty damned good. It wasn't long before he ditched most of my tutelage and began developing his own style. He was hooked.

It was cool to see him experiment with different media and begin the process of critiquing himself with every stroke of paint. So, I'm NOT the only person that does this. That's why beer's a good art accelerant. I sold several paintings from my off-hours side hustle in Dallas. This gave me a great deal of validation.

Money is freedom, and when you don't have it, life scares you more. I suppose I was validated by still having a profitable skill that I believed in. At least it was profitable in the sense that I could continue to pay for my art supplies.

Still, it was the only thing I was able to do at the time to make a buck. The failures and grit of long therapy days were repressive. Never achieving. Just grinding, pleading, struggling, and reaching. Painting was just the opposite. It was cathartic, productive, and gratifying. It made me feel like I still had value.

41

AN UNFORESEEN COMPLICATION

With two weeks left to go, I was eager to finish strong. I did an intense morning session with the physical therapist focusing primarily on my balance. I worked up quite the sweat and walked down the hall to my next appointment with the neuropsychologist. We did several logic problems and number games that became progressively more difficult and intense with each game. They all but tied knots in my brain. I developed a stabbing headache and began to feel nauseated. I took ibuprofen and drank some water. I struggled through the remainder of the session and walked across the hall to meet my occupational therapist.

The headache gripped me with such acute pain that I felt like I was going to throw up. The occupational therapist told me to call my wife. I lay on a padded therapy table with my eyes closed. My head throbbed like I'd been bludgeoned with a baseball bat. Forty minutes later, Eleni was out back. I got in her car.

"What's going on, love?" she asked.

"My head's killing me," I said. "I just need to get home and take a nap."

The drive home was nauseating and painful. The light from the midday sun pierced my eyes and poked splinters into my throbbing brain. Every micro-perturbation on the roads felt like my brain was being jarred around like a pinball. The journey home felt like the Road to Eternal Damnation.

Once home, I walked straight up to our bed and tried to take a nap. At about fifteen minutes of trying to force myself to sleep, I got the unequivocal visceral message to vomit. I moved quickly to the bathroom and began violently throwing up into the toilet. After all the contents of my breakfast were in the toilet, I then retched for another three minutes or so. I felt the back of my head. It was tense and bulging out the back of my previously opened skull hatch. I called for Eleni. I said I needed to go to a hospital. She agreed.

Nic, still working from home, came in and told us which hospital to go to. Eleni called an ambulance. Putting me in the hands of EMS professionals (and an ambulance full of medical equipment) was deemed the best course of action. Eleni jokingly said she called them to come so that I wouldn't vomit in her car. Having paid enough ambulance bills already to this point, I of course told her

I'd be fine and to just drive me there herself. She sensibly denied my request. The EMS guys came quickly and wheeled a transport stretcher into the house.

We gave them a detailed, pinpoint medical history worthy of two doctors. They got me on the stretcher after taking vital signs. I was alive, but in terrible pain. They loaded me into their ambulance and started an IV in my left arm. They hung some Lactated Ringers solution and gave me 12.5 milligrams of fentanyl. The warm rush of opiate solution in my vein was pleasantly uncomfortable and heralded some pain relief.

I finally felt a bit better, but then the nausea hit me again like a boomerang. I mumbled, "Get me a barf bag ... Now!" A green bag with a sturdy round aperture was placed beneath me. It looked like a windsock. I exorcized the latest gastric demons into this bag for five minutes or so.

I peered through the windows of the ambulance and looked on sorrowfully as Eleni and Nic got smaller in the rearview. *Here we go again*, I thought.

The ambulance transported me to a fancy hospital ER nearby with Eleni following close behind, driving her car. Upon my arrival at an ER bay, the necessary stretcher transfer felt like an M-80 going off inside my skull. I lay in pain, nauseated and deeply concerned. Had I developed a brain bleed? I wasn't so much worried that I'd had another stroke because my faculties remained intact.

The ER doc was the very caricature of an overly confident Texan. He quite literally introduced himself shooting pistol fingers in the air. Though not easily forgettable, I cannot remember his name, overshadowed as it was by his display of idiotic arrogance.

I will always remember him as "Dr. Pistol Fingers." I knew his type. I am from Texas and went to medical school in Texas. Generally, clowns like this guy never made the grades and lacked self-awareness. They also liked to wear cowboy boots in the Operating Room. There's nothing wrong with pride in your state, but when you show up hours after I've arrived without knowing my labs or vitals, you're just an incompetent jerk.

I'm a doctor. I am not some clueless patient who thinks confidence is a pair of cowboy boots that you got muddy once at your deer-hunting lease. I asked him for a CT scan, which would have been the appropriate first step.

Instead, I got an MRI. An MRI is more expensive than a CT and takes much longer to perform. This pissed me off, because I knew I was padding the coffers of the hospital administrators by agreeing to go forward. The MRI revealed no stroke or brain bleed.

Dr. Pistol Fingers then wanted to have a lumbar puncture (LP) done on me to rule out meningitis. A lumbar puncture is a spinal tap done through the low back. At this point, however, I was beginning to feel better. I had no documented fevers and my vitals were normal. My labs were normal. My MRI was normal.

I questioned this clown's motives. As Dr. Pistol Fingers had already burned the Golden Gate Bridge with me, and I was feeling better, I refused the lumbar puncture. The clown had decidedly started intravenous antibiotics on me without my knowledge and I was sent to the inpatient unit for observation. His physician's assistant was running the show from behind the scenes and was convinced I had meningitis. I'm glad she was there.

I waited several hours in the ER before being wheeled to my room. My head felt better, but it was hard to say if the pain was simply masked by opioid narcotics. Once I got settled into my hospital inpatient ward bed and the chaos subsided, the pain returned, and I started spiking fevers. The fevers made me immediately relent to the spinal tap and they sent me down to radiology to undergo the procedure. I was very much okay with an interventional radiologist sticking a needle into my spine. I was not okay with a pistol-fingered "doctor" doing it. This was probably more the reason for my initial refusal than just being stubborn.

Though not the most pleasant experience, they withdrew about ten milliliters of cerebrospinal fluid from my lumbar spine and sent it to the lab to culture it. Of course, no bacteria ultimately grew, because I was already on antibiotics thanks to Pistol Fingers. But given my immense improvement on antibacterial IV antibiotics, it was clear to me and my treating physicians that I had indeed contracted bacterial meningitis. I was treated empirically on IV antibiotics for another six days in the hospital.

On day two or so, the PICC line technician paid me a visit. As I explained earlier, a PICC line goes from a vein in your arm essentially to your heart. These are often used to deliver long-term antibiotics. The PICC technician was very cool. His job is essentially to place these things in people and nothing else. He was a shining example of practice making perfect.

Using an ultrasound, he located the basilic vein in my left

forearm and placed a large hollow needle into it. He threaded a flexible wire through it towards my heart and passed the hollow PICC line tube over the wire. He then flushed some saline through the PICC line and asked if I heard anything weird. I said indeed I did and indicated that it sounded like fluid was rushing past my left ear. He said, "Yup. It's in the wrong place."

The wire had made a wrong turn and went up my jugular vein near my left ear. He backed up the tube and, using the guide wire, found my superior vena cava as originally planned. I no longer heard the odd rush of fluid, and a subsequent X-ray confirmed the tube to be in perfect position. The PICC line was then secured to my left inner arm.

By day three my fevers had broken, and I felt great. I was clearing the meningitis that so greatly tormented my poor brain. My suspicion is that the external ventricular drain (EVD) that was initially placed in my skull caused a colony of bacteria to hang out in my cerebrospinal fluid. Being that I'm young and healthy, it probably took the little bastards all of three months to become strong and numerous enough to cause a rip-roaring infection.

My treating physicians on the floor were two Middle Eastern men of around forty and fifty years of age. They were prompt, courteous, and damn good doctors. I began to start knowing the nurses and hospital staff by name, as the insurance company drudges dragged their asses in getting me the home healthcare setup needed for the antibiotics, which I would be obliged to administer to myself.

42

MOMMA B

My favorite almost daily visitor was my housekeeper, Momma B. She was a sweet older African American woman in her sixties who always brought some cheer and candor to the room—two things that are sadly lacking in a hospital. At this point, my wife was visiting regularly and playing Rummikub with me to help pass the time. We asked Momma B what her real name was, and she said, "Beatriz. But everyone calls me Momma B." We'd always ask how she was doing, and she'd give us the God's honest truth. Somedays she'd say, "I'm great. It's been a good week." Other days maybe, "Terrible. People think they can just say whatever they want to me." She'd probably seen it all. I liked that she was upfront about things. You don't get a lot of that in hospitals either.

One day we talked with her for a while and she complimented Eleni on how pretty and well-dressed she looked. She then looked at me and said, "The doctors might call you a lot of things, but one thing you *ain't* is blind." She was a sweetheart. I came back after I was discharged to give her a nice thank-you note from my wife and me, and a gift card to a restaurant. I know her job is mostly thankless, and she probably rarely gets the praise she deserves.

43

FLYING THE COOP

Upon my discharge from the hospital, I got two soft coolers full of antibiotic pump balls with lots of IV tubing and supplies delivered to the house. We had to keep these "balls" of antibiotic solution in the refrigerator.

At 6:00 a.m., 2:00 p.m., and 10:00 p.m. every day, I had to hook up two of the ball bags of antibiotics, one from each cooler in succession, to my PICC line. They would trickle in antibiotic solution slowly. The balls were elastomeric, like water balloons slowly deflating. It took two hours to completely run in my two antibiotics. Therefore, I was going to bed at midnight and waking up at 5:00 a.m. to thaw my next dose.

Many times, I was only waking up intermittently to discover my dedicated wife hooking me up to antibiotics in the wee hours of the morning after sleeping through the alarm clock. If anyone drugs me in my sleep, I want it to be her. I had to live on this schedule with the PICC line in my arm for another two weeks.

It was early April by this time, and our employee leave was running out. Still in Dallas, Eleni needed to start work back in Albuquerque the following Monday. We loaded up, thanked our family profusely, and took off back to New Mexico. Due to the meningitis, I had been forced to miss the last week of therapy. That was not the way I had hoped to finish.

We listened to Nick Offerman's audiobook about woodworking for the lion's share of the drive. I also worked on the manuscript for this book. We talked about the things we needed to do before rejoining the rat race again. They were many, and things that would be even more onerous as we re-busied ourselves at work. I set up a required doctor's appointment to get some work release paperwork done and approved so that I could at least work in the clinic again.

I was in no way ready to do surgery yet. My left hand was still feral. At least now, though, I could stand for hours at a time when and if required. The urology chief had spoken with the administrative overlords, months in advance, to see what it was I had to get done in order to return.

The doctor's appointment was one requirement, and I had to fill out a form for a bureaucrat. Simple, right? Turns out this wasn't even a scratch on the surface of what I would ultimately have to do.

44

MEANWHILE, BACK AT THE RANCH

I returned to work in mid-April. Sort of, anyway. My service chief pulled me into his office after I saw my first patient. "We got a problem," he said. He explained that the hospital administrators had sent him an email saying I wasn't allowed to see patients. They said that before I was able to resume seeing patients, I would have to undergo a neuropsychiatric evaluation by a qualified provider and have a detailed list compiled of the things I can and cannot do at work.

Prior to returning, the original plan was for me to just resume functions as a purely clinical urologist. The plan conveyed to me was that I was to avoid doing surgical procedures until the extent of my ever-improving disabilities was fully known, at roughly a year post-injury.

I would hope this book is proof enough that my brain's ability to think and reason was largely unaffected. I don't think most stroke patients write books and paint saleable artwork immediately after their injuries. I can walk and stand for long periods at a time, as previously noted.

My poor left-hand coordination had been the only thing keeping me from being able to optimally perform surgical operations. Yet, the diagnosis and treatment of patients in the clinical setting was quite simple to me by comparison.

Nonetheless, the higher-ups were going to great lengths to cover their asses. A few years back, a surgeon in his sixties at my hospital suffered a more serious type of stroke. So serious, in fact, that he wound up with a severe expressive aphasia that rendered his spoken words into salad. He wasn't as tactful—or ethically responsible—as I, and he began operating again whether people liked it or not.

It caused an uproar, and the guy was ultimately escorted off the premises by security. Thus, the administrators were more than likely trying to avoid a similar situation.

What they failed to understand is that my situation is entirely different. Regardless, I had become a prisoner again. If I lashed out, I would be seen as angry and impulsive. I would be seen as displaying a collection of symptoms of a disease process common to brain-injured adults. Yes, they were justified in throwing out a guy who was acting unethically and unprofessionally, whether he knew it or not. However, I came at this, from the beginning, with the intention to *"primum non nocere"* ("First, do no harm").

My left hand is shit. I can't operate right now at my best. Patients deserve only my best. I'm not in the business of being an unethical ass at the expense of hurting someone. I was up front about that, and thus we made a plan, months before my return. I still have a lot of value as a clinical urologist, and my recovery is still in evolution.

Tell me I'm useless a year from now; that may turn out to be true. Tell me I'm useless now and henceforth indefinitely; that cannot be confirmed. Brain injuries are not static. I was benched from helping out the team. Our practice was already down to just three of us, and now I was being pulled from the team to sit behind a desk to field computer consults and do paperwork.

I resolved to persevere, but trying to get a neuropsychologist to see me quickly was a mountain to move in itself. Many of my doctors didn't want the burden of responsibility for assessing whether I could or couldn't go back to work. The "doctor" I had originally been required to see before returning to my job had given me the go-ahead to proceed with clinical duties after doing a full neurologic exam. He agreed that I could return immediately to clinical duties and to work out a proctored, gradual return to performing surgical procedures.

He was, however, a nurse practitioner, and my employer didn't recognize his credentials. But look: I didn't get to choose who saw me after my stroke. I was placed with him, *and* the fact of the matter is that nurse practitioners in New Mexico can legally practice independently. It's not my fault if my hospital cannot join the twenty-first century.

Furthermore, the hospital that took my insurance wasn't even doing neuro-psych evaluations, citing COVID as the reason. This virus' slogan should be "COVID: Preventing people from doing any work since 2020." The fact was that I needed a neuro-psych evaluation from someone whose credentials my hospital employers "recognized." If a given institution wasn't doing certain procedures due to outside pressures, well . . .

As a physician, I pulled every string and favor I had in town to get an appointment with a private-practice neuropsychologist about two weeks after my initial "start" date had passed. In the meantime, I uselessly sat behind a desk doing a drone's work.

A neuropsychiatric evaluation is a standardized four- to six-hour test. When I arrived at the evaluation, I didn't care how long the eval would take, but I certainly wanted to know how long it would take to get the results. So I asked the doc. He said four to six weeks. I said I didn't have that kind of time. It was the truth: our clinic was already backlogged due to COVID and we were essentially down to only two providers. He said he was going on vacation to Hawaii the following week. Good for him. But I was the one being coerced into submitting to the timeline of a vacationing shrink. Also, I was paying this guy two hundred bucks an hour out of pocket so that he could test my cognition to see if I was fit to return to work. I felt helpless at the time, but it wasn't his fault. True, I would not have dropped a pre-planned vacation for a patient's sake either, but I do have partners. In such a situation, I probably would have found a way to get things done.

I needed a form signed and a letter written to return to work. I could feel the all-too-familiar overwhelming sense of a long road ahead. Head held low, I returned to my clinic with the news. After another five weeks of being a desk jockey, I returned nervously for the neuro-psych testing. As you can imagine, I'm no stranger to tests, but this one was by far the most nerve-racking. There was a lot on the line.

The evaluation was difficult. To be under the microscope that long is challenging in itself. In addition, the shrink made it clear I would be held to a higher standard. He said he'd assume my IQ was roughly one hundred twenty given I was a physician. I'd be held to that standard.

If I failed, my career would be gone in a flash. Two hundred thousand dollars of debt, four years of medical school, and five years of residency. All for naught. All flushed down the toilet. No pressure.

I'd love to see a hospital administrator take this test—and see the results! It was a bear. Nonetheless, I struggled through it. I had no choice. Being a drug-dealing doctor for a New Mexican queenpin was sounding better and better. Why was I being treated like a pariah?

45

CLEAR FOR TAKEOFF

With the odds stacked against me, I passed the lengthy neuropsychiatric evaluation. Additionally, my neurologist from the Stroke Team at my treating hospital evaluated me through a thorough exam, and at last, I was cleared to return to clinical duties. Surgeries would have to wait.

At least I was going to see patients again. I returned to clinical duties as soon as I was permitted. I was glad to be back at work. The first patient I saw was sitting in the procedure hallway awaiting results. Accompanied by his wife, he was a patient of mine that I hadn't seen in four or five months. "Dr. Choate, how are you, buddy? You look great," he said.

Somehow, he had found out that I had been hospitalized with a stroke, and I remembered he had gone to the effort of sending me a card, which I read in the step-down hospital. I received several cards from friends and family, but I'll never forget that this patient's card found its way to me despite the COVID gestapo. We were glad to see each other. Tears welled up in his reddening eyes. "I am so relieved you're okay," he said. I thanked him and his wife for the card and gave him a big hug. We were both fighting back tears.

It was not the welcome back I'd anticipated, but it was truly special and reminded me of why I love this job. Getting back in the swing of clinic was easy compared to the ordeal I'd just been through. If anything, I was better than I was before. All the logic problems and critical thinking exercises I had done in speech therapy sharpened my brain. I was also better at empathy.

I no longer guessed at how people felt when they were critically ill. I no longer pretended to know what a catheter felt like. I knew in painstaking, lucid detail what my patients were going through, and I could level with them. I was no longer an imposter shouting orders from a tower of superior immortality.

I still continue to do physical and occupational therapy in Albuquerque. They probably think I have a screw loose, being that I'm back to basic functioning yet keep showing up for the next session. They are used to teaching people how to walk again or do chores around the house. I see them gasp when I tell them that last weekend I built a brick and mortar retaining wall, or that I hiked two miles to go fly-fishing. I'm not their average octogenarian patient.

I know they realize I'm young and had a life of high function—a life that I'm ever-striving to regain in full—but I don't think they always know what to do with me. Nonetheless, I have a great team of caring therapists that push me to be better. As a result, the frame through which I view my goals has shifted. I'm no longer working solely towards personal goals like walking my dog or making dinner.

I'm now working and fighting to be better for those in my life. I want the best for Eleni. I want the best for my family. I want the best for my patients, and I know I'll never get there by sitting on the sidelines. Motivations will change, but as long as we support them with our actions, the sky's the limit.

46

LOOKING OUTWARD MEANS LOOKING INWARD

After living through this hell, my perspective on life has changed. Not that I did much before, but I no longer put much stock in hope. Hope is a delusion of gamblers. Regrets, however, are the choices we make. We all want to be in control of our own destinies. Those who loathe responsibility will even choose to live their lives by accepting the notion that "everything happens for a reason."

Maybe so, but those reasons are often absurd if you think existence is preordained. Child soldiers who are slain before their eleventh birthday happen for a reason. I don't think you can hope your way into a bright future, but rather just stay sharp, lean, and proactive: doing all you have to do so that you won't look back on your life with regret. Life is too short for that.

Looking back, I completed months of therapy and for some reason chose to undertake a very expensive, intensive stroke rehab program ten hours away from my beloved home. I hate Dallas. Eleni and I slept on a twin bed without box springs for a month to attend this program. I suppose the reason I chose to do this was not that I blissfully assumed it would fix me. I did it because I didn't want to look back in six months and think, *Damn, I could have been doing surgery by now had I attended that program.* I did not want to dismiss a treatment opportunity that might go some measure toward improving the lot of my career and personal life. There's no way to have known at the time if there was even a chance of that.

That's living in the past. That's not healthy for the brain or the heart. "You miss one hundred percent of the shots you don't take," said Wayne Gretzky, or maybe it was Michael Jordan. I've now completed the program, and I still have an Everest to climb to get back to normal. However, I'm starting on the mountain. I'm not stuck at an airport bound for Nepal.

I sleep well at night. I don't ruminate regretting whether or not I should have done something. It may be said, I took a shot, but I failed, and I regret it. At times, this can seem like the only rational response, but I think it's definitely much easier to think about things you could have done differently, adjust, and try, try again.

It's more devastating to have to regret having not taken any action whatsoever. This tends to ignite an explosion of hypotheticals that seem to infest the brain to no limit. What if I had done this? What if I had done that? *Shut your mouth, brain. I'm trying to sleep, so I can take care of you.*

Inactivity is a drug that the human brain has developed over thousands of years of evolution. I killed a mastodon last Thursday, so I don't need to go out and risk my life today to feed my family. With the exponential opportunities created by modern digital technology, many forms of inactivity have never been easier.

We don't even have to date formally anymore to vet potential partners. I met my wife on Bumble, but I still felt compelled to meet up with her at a brewery in person. Boy, am I glad I didn't chicken out on that. I might otherwise be alone, without love, or even dead right now.

A friend in medical school once told me that her attending physician said that "motivation follows action." Damn, is that true. This book is a prime example. I can now type thirty-six words per minute. I started at twenty-four. You may laugh at that, but it's important to me. My livelihood depends on it.

If you're ever at a crossroads in life, think of action as the tokens you must drop into the arcade game to get started. Real motivation comes with taking ownership of that action. The outcome, good or bad, happens. You own it, though. So, you either reap the rewards of that action or learn from a bad outcome, from which should arise the motivation to move on to something else.

We also learn from others' actions all the time, but we can't always rely on them for everything. Some situations are too unique to have been experienced by them. Therefore, sometimes we just have to grab the bull by the horns, as they say. I want to stare down adversity and do more with eighty percent of a brain than most people do with a whole one.

I often wonder if the human condition of suffering is merely a rite of passage. A toll for having a go at life. Are we meant to be half-capable at some point? Are we meant to have our futures muddied? Is life a gift, a curse, or some evolutionary state of fact? Regardless, I'm afraid of what heaven will demand. As a self-proclaimed self-aware individual, knowing that someone has it worse off is less a comfort than a prison. Perhaps speaking only of the stroke community itself, there are people affected by strokes that cannot lead the life they once had, and there are people that essentially no longer have a life without the constant support of family members and healthcare workers. Yet, just because some people with strokes didn't experience the most extreme outcome, this doesn't make their newfound problems meaningless. I still constantly think about my neurological limitations and become frustrated when I can't do the things I once did effortlessly. Though grave, my present condition would be classified by my Great Depression-surviving grandmother as "pissing and moaning." Rather befitting for a guy that treats kidney stones. Yet, I suppose nowadays it's commonplace for people to gripe about anything. As a physician, the people that are "worse off" with whom I've seen and developed relationships endure plights stranger than fiction. Imagine not being able to stand. Not being able to kiss or make love. Imagine having a stroke that takes away the use of your dominant hand. Takes away your ability to speak or see. Many people don't have to imagine this. They live it every day. I grew up hearing how blessed I was. I unfortunately never focused much on that. Instead, I focused on my shortcomings. How easily depressed I got. How I wasn't as popular or rich as other kids. How I drank too much at parties to quell anxiety. How little I felt like I could relate to anyone. It's cliché to say you don't know what you've got 'til it's gone, but I'll be damned if that ain't the truth. I realize now that I should have been more thankful for what I had, what I earned, and what I had the potential to do. And yet, I waited for lightning to strike me down.

My dad has a neurosurgeon buddy living in Dallas that he grew up with playing little league baseball. Over the course of my treatment, unbeknownst to me, he had been reviewing my hospital course and giving my dad his opinion of how things were going, especially when things seemed like they weren't. My dad suggested I call him while I was in rehab in Dallas, as he'd been asking about me lately.

I called him up nervously one evening to thank him for all the help and support. I imagined how tedious it must have been for him to have to translate medical jargon and imaging results for my dad every night.

He is a really good guy. He told me that less than a year ago, he had fainted from the side effects of a prescription medication, causing him to land forcefully on the floor. Frozen by years of the strain of performing lengthy surgeries, his neck hyperextended from the fall, resulting in a cervical spine injury. He woke up knowing he'd be a quadriplegic. He was unfortunately correct. At least temporarily anyway. He had just retired after a full career.

He said, about midway through the first year, he wanted to kill himself. I'd be lying if I said that thought never occurred to me as well. At one low point, he confided to one of his neurosurgery partners that he simply didn't want to live that way any longer. He was dependent on assistance for pretty much everything. His partner urged him to just give it more time and do more rehab. He agreed, then put in the work. Now, almost a year out, he told me how excited he was to get to play his first season of golf.

We talked about the changing landscape of medicine and how physician burnout is getting a lot of attention these days. He told me that despite that side of the story, we as physicians are truly blessed to get to care for people regardless of their age, race, gender, or ability to pay. To be able to help people who have placed their trust in us, there's no greater joy, he asserted. He's right. He said, "Keep fighting. Look the black abyss in the eye and say fuck you!" After essentially being told he'd never walk again, he persevered. He was going to return to something he loved doing once again. He told me to follow the same path as he had, and to not give up. I have not. He had no regrets putting in the work. Neither do I.

ABOUT THE AUTHOR

Dr. Bevan Choate is a urologist, artist, and author of *The Stroke Artist*, a story that speaks to all who have, at one time or another, faced and then overcome life's unplanned obstacles. Just when Dr. Choate had found his stride as a successful surgeon, he suffered a stroke, and the music stopped. Overnight, he went from the ship's captain to a passenger floating aimlessly at sea. His story is one of grit and the determination to be better—despite the odds. Dr. Choate received his medical doctorate from Texas Tech Health Sciences Center and completed a five-year residency through the University of New Mexico Hospitals. He now lives in Albuquerque, New Mexico, with his wife and dog Indi and pursues painting, fly-fishing, and urology.

ACKNOWLEDGEMENTS

Writing a book is like climbing a mountain. It's challenging but fulfilling when the destination is finally reached. Producing a readable book and seeing it through to publication is a lot like moving the mountain you just climbed. Doing this all while trying to recover from a life-threatening stroke, to many, may seem odd. But I don't think I could have done it any other way.

Moving a mountain takes a village. A village of truly selfless and compassionate souls without whom I wouldn't have made half the incredible progress I have made thus far. In no particular order, I would like to give special thanks to the following people. (Forgive me in advance if I have left anyone out. Cut me some slack. I only have 80 percent of a brain.)

To my childhood author hero John Erickson. I've said not infrequently that without your book series I'd be illiterate. That may be hyperbolic, but I will add that perhaps I would not have found reading to be a fun endeavor early on without your gift of storytelling. You inspired me to push this thing through and get it published by a real outfit.

Allan Harris. We are both half-cowboy, half-artist. The world needs more of us, and I thank you for your love and support.

To Perry Flippin. A little help from a real writer and editor goes a long way in the mind of a young, new author and for that I thank you.

Jordan Brady, MD. My co-resident, wild stallion, and brother in the battlefield of a five-year urology residency. You told me to write this damn book and look where we are now. I wasn't real excited at the time, but I'm glad you held my feet to the fire.

My uncle Guy. Without your edits early on, this book may have never gotten off the ground. Thank you for giving me the confidence to move forward with a polished work.

To my late grandparents Martha and Wade, without whom I would not be half the man I am today.

To my parents, Vic and Cathy, and my sister and her family. I love you all. Your support through all this has kept me going and given me a second chance at a good life.

To my Greek parents Maria and George. Thank you for giving me a loving home, a warm bed, and many excellent dinners during the Great Freeze of 2021.

Nic, Seraphina, and Marianna. I would not have wanted to spend my early stroke recovery with any other family. Thank you all for making stroke recovery as fun as it could be.

Acknowledgements

To the people of San Angelo, Texas. Without you raising, loving, and supporting me, I would not have gone so far. Thank you.

My friends in Albuquerque who worked a tremendous amount both behind and in the scenes of my recovery. I thank you with all my heart. Thank you, Jordan, Trevor, Cameron, Michelle, Matt, and Anna. You guys helped my wife and me through some hard times. Cheers.

To Mike Martinez, Sharon Lewis, David Robbins, and Tony Smith. My urology family who held down the fort during my tour of various hospitals. You mean more to me than you guys know.

To the wonderful urology nurses and health technicians with whom I work every day. You make me happy to come to work.

The university hospital members who brought me back to life deserve my strongest possible endorsement. To the nurses, doctors, technicians, residents, and advanced practice providers who cared for me at the university hospital. I am forever grateful.

To all of my wonderful physical, occupational, and speech therapists in Albuquerque. You are the unsung heroes who move the needle. Thank you.

Thank you to my LTAC caregivers who put in the hard work to bring me back to the land of the living.

Thank you to the Baylor Scott & White Day Neuro Program. Your prowess is unparalleled. Your team is fantastic and allowed me to make great strides.

To my cousin Michael and my San Angelo buddies. Thank you

for keeping me grounded, sane, and giving me something to look forward to.

Indi. My anxious and loving cow dog. I am glad you are still with us, and I'm glad to be greeted by you every morning.

To my dad's friend and neurosurgeon, Hunt. Thank you for your patience and expertise. Your words and past experiences were truly inspiring and helped me overcome some tough times.

Finally, I want to thank the Greenleaf Book Group and the team who worked tirelessly with me to realize this project. They were professional in the highest sense of the word. Without you all, this would not have been what it is. I truly appreciate you all.

www.ingramcontent.com/pod-product-compliance
Lightning Source LLC
Chambersburg PA
CBHW060522080526
44586CB00012B/579